Nel mezzo del cammin di nostra vita
mi ritrovai per una selva oscura
ché la diritta via era smarrita.

Midway on our life's journey,
I found myself in dark woods,
the right road lost.

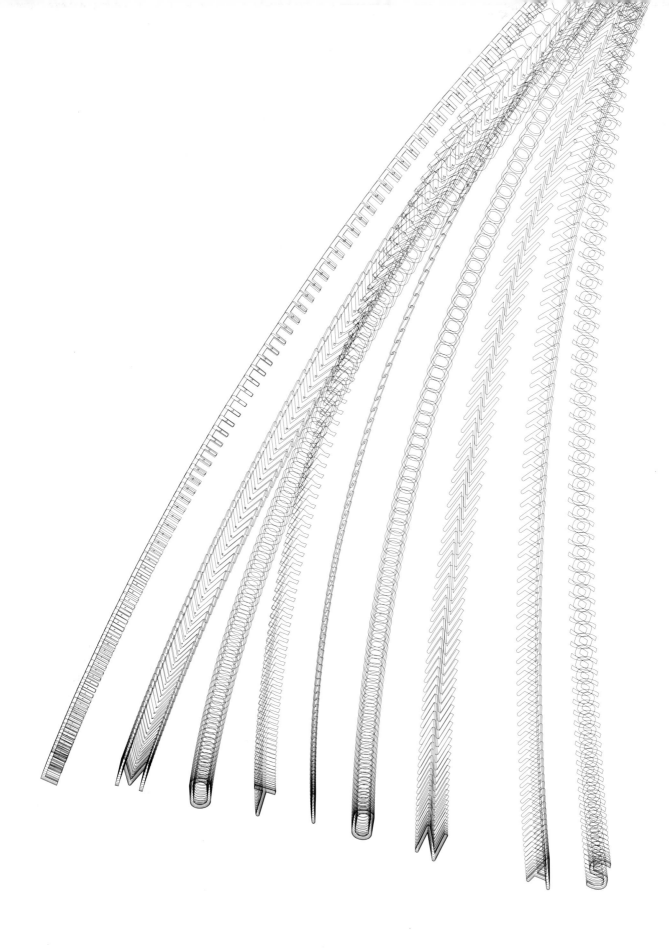

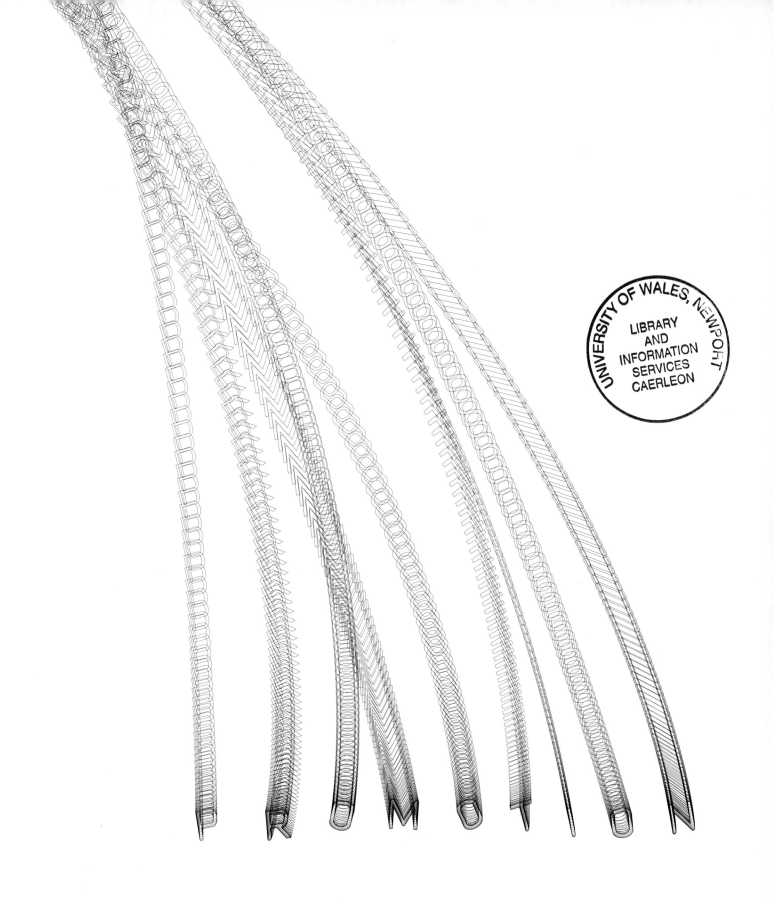

A book of Thirst edited by Rick Valicenti

THE MONACELLI PRESS

First published in the United States of America in 2005 by
The Monacelli Press, Inc.
902 Broadway, New York, New York 10010.

Copyright © 2005 The Monacelli Press, Inc.

Library of Congress Cataloging-in-Publication Data
Emotion as promotion : a book of Thirst / edited by Rick Valicenti.
p.   cm.
ISBN 1-58093-097-2
1. Valicenti, Rick—Themes, motives. 2. Thirst (Firm)—Themes, motives. I. Valicenti, Rick. II. Thirst (Firm).
NC999.4.V35A4 2001
741.6'092—dc21   2001044783

Printed and bound in China

This book was designed using Adobe® InDesign®. The publisher is grateful to Adobe Systems, Inc., for technical support.

Designed by Thirstype
Typeset in Infinity, designed by Rick Valicenti & chester

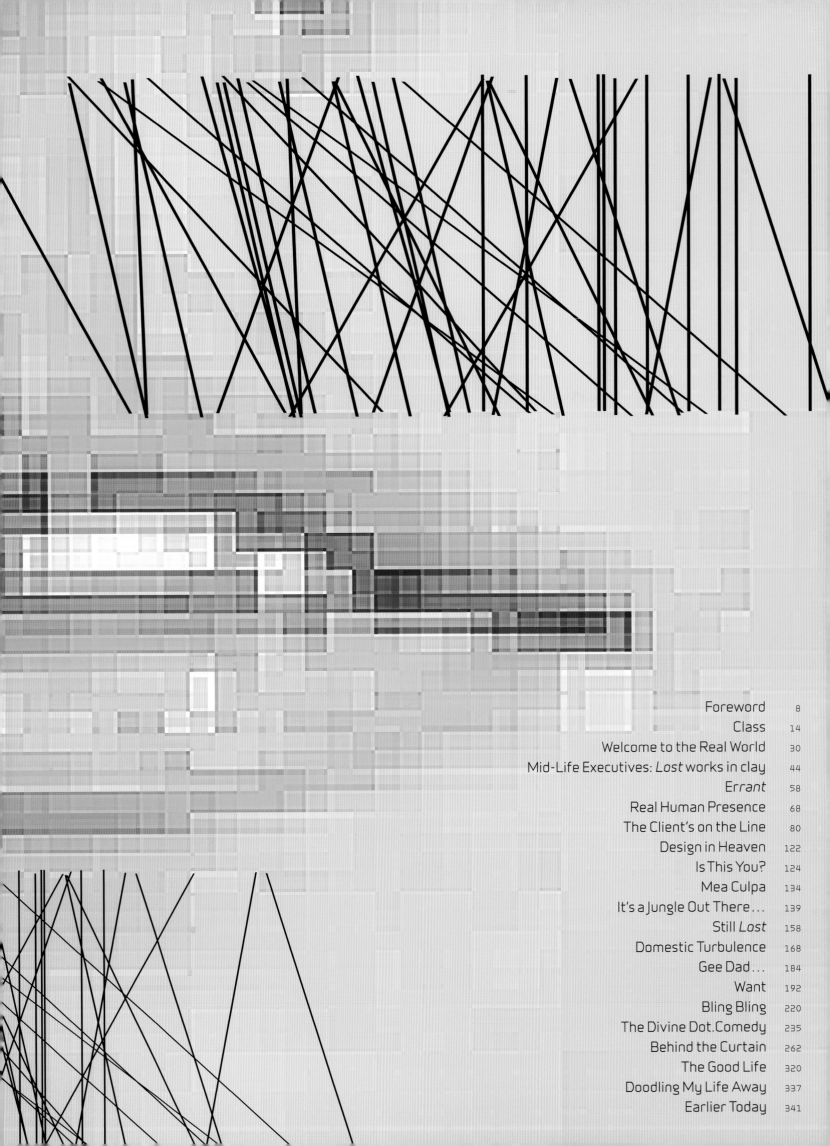

To those who take **it** personally.

3ST	IN COLLABORATION 1989–2003
EA	EDDIE ADAMS
SA	SARAH ARMBRUSTER
MB	MARIAN BANTJES
CB	CHRIS BLAKE
TJB	TJ BLANCHFLOWER
DB	DAKOTA BROWN
GB	GREGG BROKAW
C	CHESTER
MD	MATT DALY
BD	BARRY DECK
RD	ROB DEWEY
ND	NIKOLA DJUREK
JE	JASON EISELE
AE	ANN EVANSON
CE	CLIFF EVANSON
FF	FRANK FORD
MG	MICHAEL GIAMMANCO
PG	PATRICK GIASSON
RH	RICH HANSON
JH	JULIE HOLCOMB
LH	LISA HUGHES
MH	MILENA HUGHES
RI	ROB IRRGANG
RJ	RON JACOMINI
TJ	TRACY JENKINS
CJ	CHAD JOHNSTON
GK	GEOFF KAPLAN
K	KAZU
PK	PATRIC KING
TK	TONY KLASSEN
PK2	PETRA KLUSMEYER
IK	ILSE KRAUSE
DL	DAVID LADWIG
TL	TODD LIEF
ML	MICHAEL LOPEZ
MM	MOULI MARUR
JM	JOYCE MAST
BM	BRIAN McMULLEN
AEM	ANDREA E. MONFRIED
YM	YOLANDA MORAN
GM	GREGORY MURPHY
MP	MICHAEL PAPPAS
HPA	HARSH PATEL
RP	RICHARD PAUL
CP2	CHARLIE PETERSON
CP	CORRINE PFISTER
CP3	CHUCK PLOCKMEYER
JP	JOHN POBOJEWSKI
HP	HEATHER PRIEST
MR2	MAGNUS RAKENG
MR	MARK RATTIN
KR	KEN REID
FR	FRANCOIS ROBERT
JR	JIM ROOT
ES	EWA SARNACKA
ES2	ED SCHWEITZER
TS2	TOM SINNOTT
VS	VICTOR SKREBNESKI
ES3	ERIN SMITH
JNS	JAMES NOEL SMITH
TS	TOM STANDAGE
PS	PAUL SYCH
TT	TRACY TAYLOR
TT2	TIM TURNER
TV	TOM VACK
BV	BARBARA VALICENTI
LQV	LINDA Q. VALICENTI
LV	LYNDON VALICENTI
NV	NONI VALICENTI
RV	RICK VALICENTI
SV	SONNY VALICENTI
WV	WILLIAM VALICENTI
NV2	NICK VEASEY
GV	GINA VIECELI
VV	VELLO VIRKHAUS
RW3	RICHARD WEAVER
RW2	ROB WEAVER
RW4	RICHARD WHITE
RW	ROB WITTIG
AW	ALICE WORLD
YY	YOONJUNG YANG
JY	JIM YORK

SEE HOW WE LIVE.

...sometimes you're the reflection...

...and sometimes you're the provider.

SERV-US

Schmervice

So should you care enough to practice design,
may I offer a few tried-and-true lessons
that sustain creative joy and the illusion of…
design, the noble profession.

Enter:

CLASS

Foster Trust and Confidence

Lesson 2
Voice Transcendence

Lesson 3
Encourage Unbridled Zeal

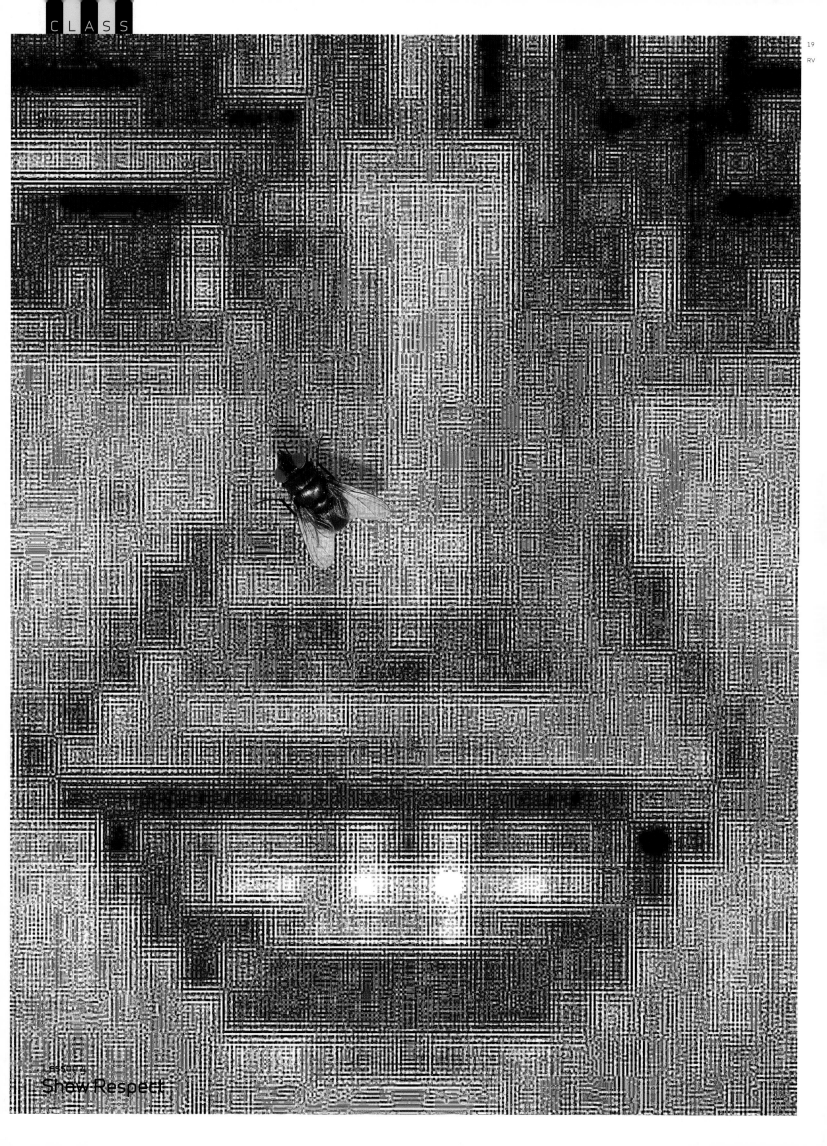

Lesson 9
Show Respect

Lesson 6
Practice Self-Control

Listen Carefully, Then Lead

Lesson 8
Be Seductive

Reflect a Sense of Humor

Lesson 10
Embrace Incredibly Talented Friends

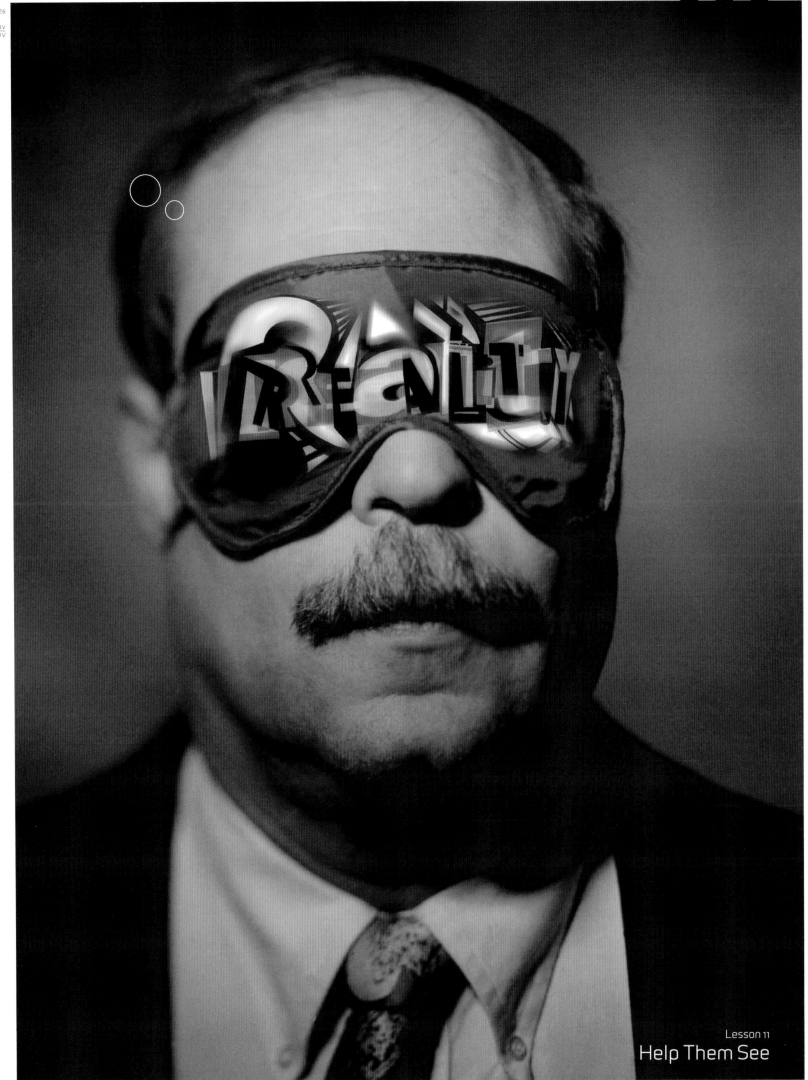

Lesson 11
Help Them See

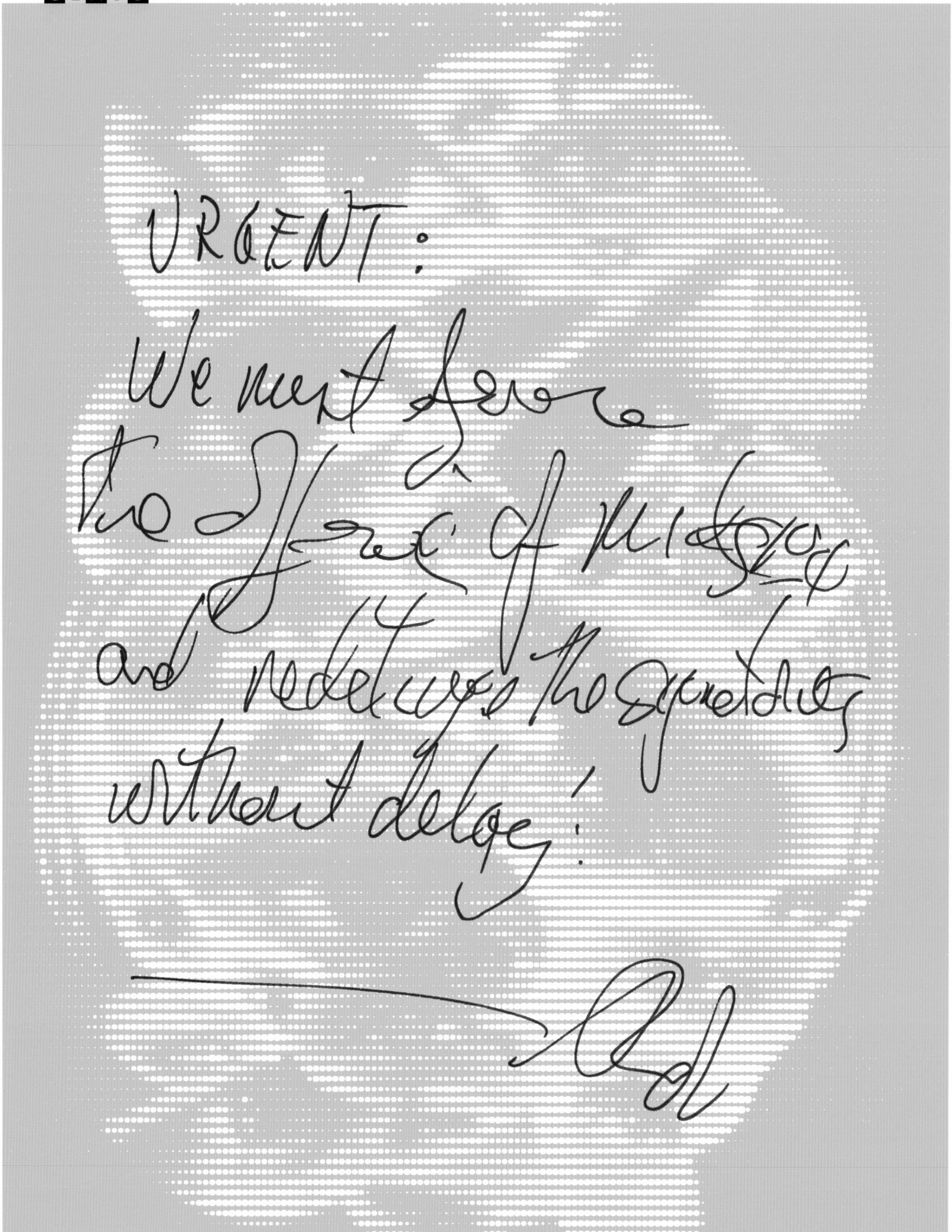

URGENT:

We must devote
the Short of midway
and redeploy the squadrons
without delay!

Lesson 12
Get It in Writing

Class Dismissed

REMEMBER WHAT YOU JUST LEARNED. NEVER STOP REMINDING YOURSELF THAT DESIGN *IS A NOBLE PURSUIT* AND *SOME DAYS ARE BETTER THAN OTHERS*

Go forth and multitask.

Welcome to the Real World

Within a five-mile radius of my home,
forty miles outside of Chicago,
independently owned retail establishments
display evidence of the original modernist ideals:
simplicity, universality, consistency.

Unwittingly, the presence of humanity has been stripped;
unknowingly, design apathy has been highlighted.
Helvetica Bold equals excellent legibility at cruising speed.
Orange Plexiglas equals minimal nocturnal blur.
Coming soon to a neighborhood near you…

GOODS

AND

SERVICES

REAL
SPECIALTIES
CARPET
TRAVEL
USED CARS
LAUNDRY
BEEF
CANDIES

-HR PHOTO

24 HOUR PHARMACY

BOOKSTORE

CLEANERS

COMMUNITY

CURRENCY EXCHANGE

DOCTOR

DRUG FOOD

EXIT

FITNESS

FOOTWEAR

LAW OFFICES

LINENS

POOL

THRIFT

VIDEO

WATERBEDS

WEIGHT

VARIETY
ABUNDANCE
CHOICE
SELECTION
BOUNTY

IKIDO AUTO BATHS BEDDING

CHIROPRACTOR CHOP SUEY COMPUTERS CONSIGNMENT

DANCE DOGS FAMOUS
OUNTRYSIDE

FLORIST FOOD GOLF GYROS

HOBBIES JEWELERS 진미식품 LIMOUSINE

LIQUORS MOO OIL CHANGE PAPER

PARTY PET FOOD PIZZA RAMA

REAL ESTATE RESTAURANT SUNTAN SUSHI

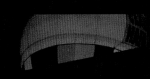

"RICK. YOU ARE MY FATHER." ONCE SAID A BRIGHT YOUNG STUDENT ASSISTANT.

39
RV
BM

Outsiders might develop a sense that Rick leads Thirst as something of a self-styled Skywalker. For him, the design world is an epic, family-oriented, Manichaean struggle. He designs by The Force, kid sister at his side, handful of colorful teammates on call. His mission is to remain one of the necessarily few against-the-odds rebels.

But over a lunch Rick bought us one day, I discovered that it is the "dark side" of design — the de facto design empire of Orange Plexiglas Helvetica Bold — that history might point to as the root of Thirst.

In 1978 Rick inadvertently fell into his first major responsibility: the identity redesign for Jewel, a vast Chicagoland supermarket chain. (Could it be, or become, his most ubiquitous work?)

That year the Ryder Type Gallery sponsored an exhibition, "Postmodern Typography," curated by Bill Bonnell, design director of the Container Corporation of America. Rick visited the show more than once and reveled in the inventive, self-expressive work of Wolfgang Weingart and April Greiman: "I had no idea there was this world of 'real' design out there."

At the time a young, unschooled production assistant to Bruce Beck, Rick was to assist in the production of Bruce's ideas for a new Jewel identity direction. All of Bruce's treatments were, in the tradition of Jewel's existing identity, explicitly friendly.

In response to the "Postmodern Typography" show, Rick underscored the word "Jewel" in Helvetica bold italic: "I drew the word 'Jewel' because it was on my mind."

When Bruce needed a thirteenth design to present to Jewel during the corporation's market research process, Rick showed Bruce his blocky experiment and Bruce snatched it up as a sure-fire loser.

Who would have expected that Rick's logo sketch, unanimously hated by focus groups, would seduce the Jewel leadership with the illusion of the fast, the new, the now? Who would have imagined that a sketch born of curiosity and playfulness could amount to something like this?

"Da Jewel is my design curse," Rick chuckles.

I wonder if that's true. If the Jewel logotype really is Rick's curse, why would he allow one to stare and yell into the left side of his face every day? How could he endure sitting one foot away from a pane of glass that frames one of those glowering orange masses as perfectly as these pages frame its 1980 prototype photograph?

One of three answers I'll make up is that Thirst's proximity to Jewel is a coincidence. I have never seen Rick stare or yell back at the Jewel. And around here, Jewel stores are everywhere.

Another answer is that Rick thrives on "curses." The Jewel's presence might remind him — if and when he needs a reminder — to make Thirst's work count, since it just might affect the visual landscape of millions of human beings.

Yet another answer, perhaps the most revealing, is that the Jewel design experience is a fond memory for Rick. Despite the outcome, the process probably fed his understanding of what it means to be a designer whose expectations deny discoveries.

Brian McMullen
Indiana University '01
design assistant to Rick Valicenti/Thirst

$.99 US

$.99 US

$1.15 US

$1.65 US

$1.69 US

$1.69 US

$1.79 US

$1.99 US

$2.15 US

$2.49 US

$2.57 US

$2.79 US

$2.99 US

$3.15 US

$3.15 US

$3.50 US

$3.79 US

$4.35 US

DESIGN IS GOOD FOR BUSINESS: REDUCED FAT VS. FAT-FREE_2003

$.50 us

$.79 us

$.85 us

$1.15 us

$1.43 us

$1.49 us

$1.69 us

$1.65 us

$1.65 us

$2.19 us

$2.45 us

$2.45 us

$2.75 us

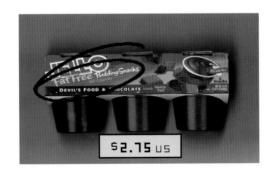

$2.75 us

$2.99 us

$3.25 us

$3.99 us

$3.99 us

Mid-Life Executives: *Lost* works in clay

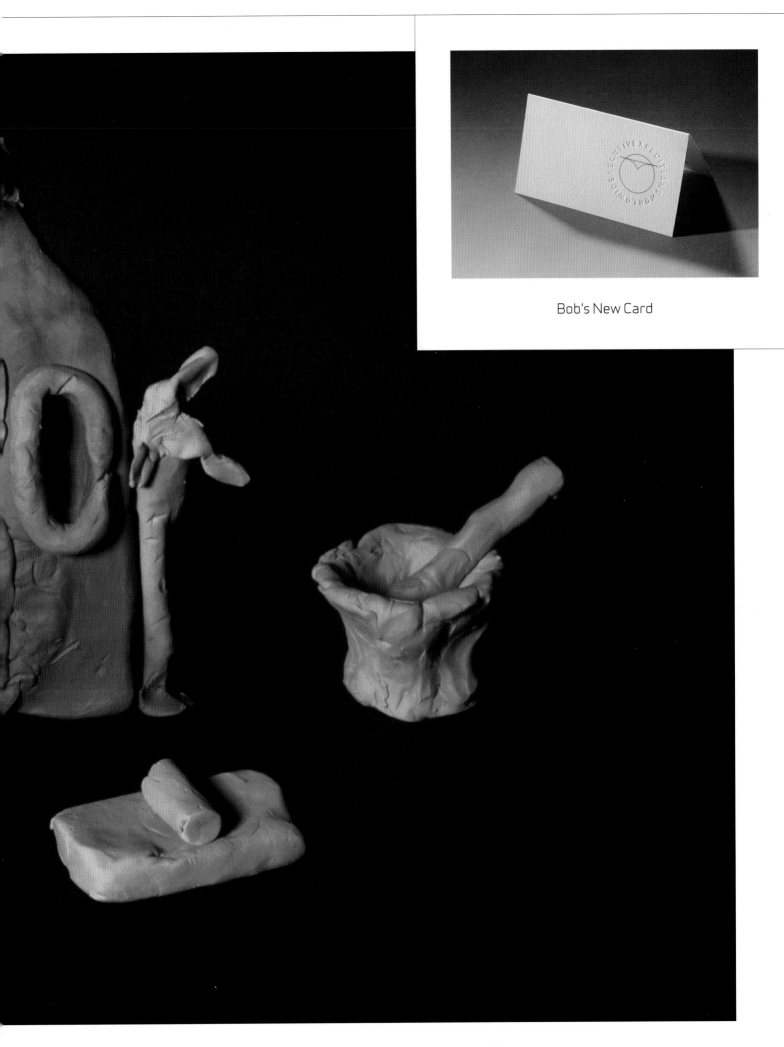

Bob's New Card

Accessorized Home for Two with One Entrance

Huh? May I ask who's calling?

My name is Bob. I found your name in the Yellow Pages under design. I'm looking to have a business card designed. Do you do business cards?

Well, as part of much larger programs, in conjunction with…yes. I guess the answer is yes, I do business cards.

Okay, good, when can we meet?

Ah, oh mmmm, what kind of business is this for?

Well, I'm a psychologist.

Are you looking for new patients?

Not exactly, I have enough clients.

Then why do you need a card?

Harvard University has invited me to give a weekend workshop. It'll be for alumni who have achieved CEO-like status within their organizations and have discovered that there must be more than work and status in life.

Please continue.

Well, that's about it. I need a card for a handful of participants.

Mmmm, what kind of clients do you normally keep?

Only men.

Men?

Yes, men who have reached the top of the corporate ladder and feel somewhat *lost*.

I can relate. What do you do for them?

I meet with them once a week to talk and twice a year I engage them in an executive expedition.

Oh, like Outward Bound?

Not exactly.

Then what? Oh, and please excuse me for asking. I assume I'm doing a business card, so I just want to have a little more context for the design.

That's okay. For the last expedition I sent each of them an address. An address to a place out West. It was actually an invitation. Time, date, etc. When they all arrived, of course none of them knew each other. But they each knew me. I proceeded to take their cell phones, luggage, wallets, credit cards, all of those things. Then I gave them each an apple, a quarter, and a map to our next destination, which was five hundred miles away.

Wow.

I told them they could either go it alone or join together in a buddy system. For the first time in a long time these men were without any support staff. Nothing!

What did they do?

Well, two days later they all showed up at the next spot. It was the base of a mountain, and there they found a map to an alpine cabin five thousand feet up. It was interesting. They ate uneaten pizza off of Pizza Hut tables and they earned transportation money by going to the local newspaper, to write and edit copy.

How enterprising! So what do you have in store for the next group? For the Harvard grads?

A number of exercises. None will be outdoors, but all the exercises will fall outside their expectations. During the weekend, they will each be coronated. And also asked to sculpt their identity in clay.

Clay?

The thing about clay is you don't have to be an artist. Clay gives them the opportunity to express themselves in a direct and simple fashion. Everyone will do fine. At the end I will fire their sculptures and give them to them to keep.

Okay. I think we should meet and talk some more. I'll do your card while you're here. It will be a pleasure. 8:30 tomorrow, here?

Fine. I've got the address here.

As I begin to process all of this, Bob, is there anything else I should know?

Not really. I'm a Vietnam vet. My personal sign is the Black Tiger. I raise horses and my daughter is thirteen.

Mmmm, my son is thirteen and I have referred to my professional practice approach as the White Tiger.

We seem to have found ourselves on an interesting parallel plane. I look forward to meeting you.

The clay sculptures, by the way. Do you think I could arrange for them to be photographed, documented, before you have them fired?

Well, nobody has ever asked for that. If my clients remain anonymous, I don't see why not.

TEMPUS FUGIT…

Bob's business card is finally designed and engraved. The Harvard alumni weekend happens in Phoenix and the photographs of the sculptures are in hand.

Before the day-old sculptures can be fired, they are inadvertently thrown out by the resort hotel that is hosting Bob and company.

The following pages present the only record of "Mid-Life Executives: *Lost* works in clay."

Disembodied Hand with Sphere

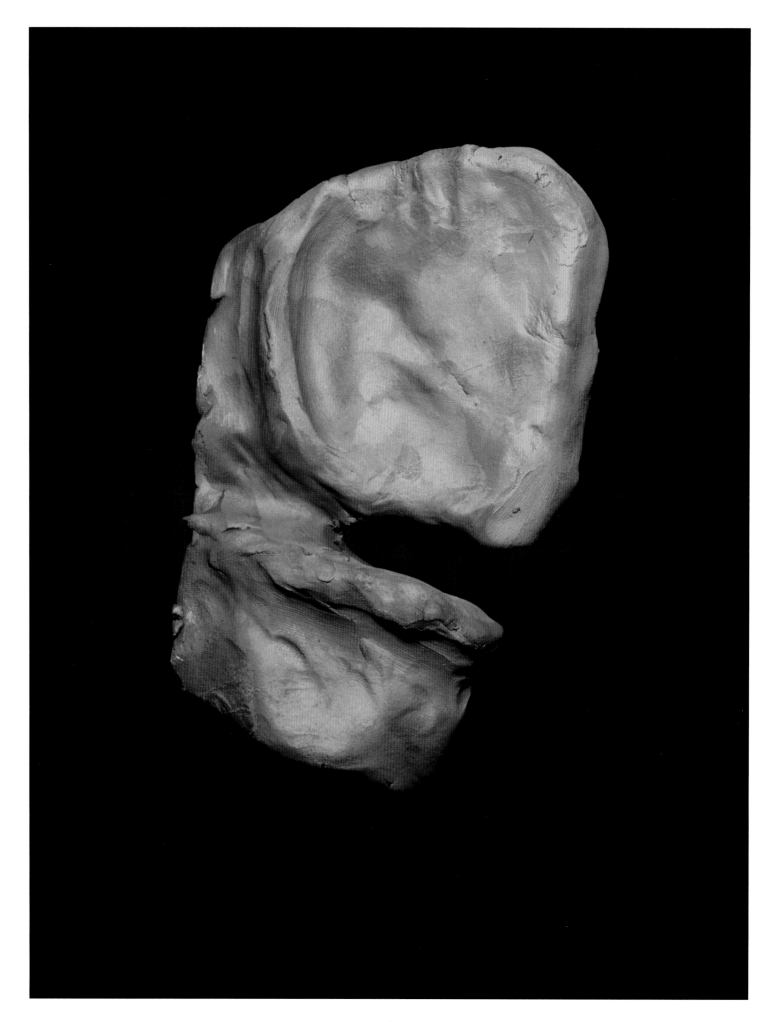

Face/Tool

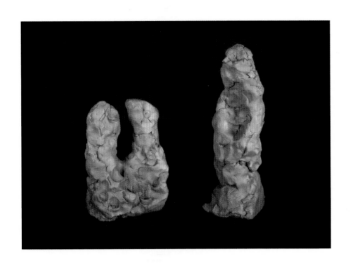

Two Conjoined Figures Facing Single Figure

Still Life with Generic Objects

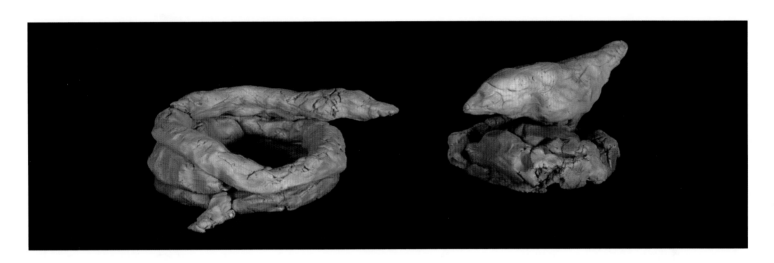

Standoff

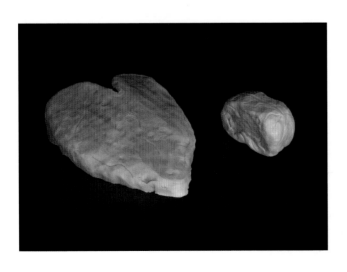

Heart and Lump

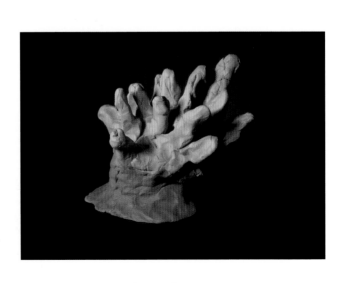

Spiderfingers

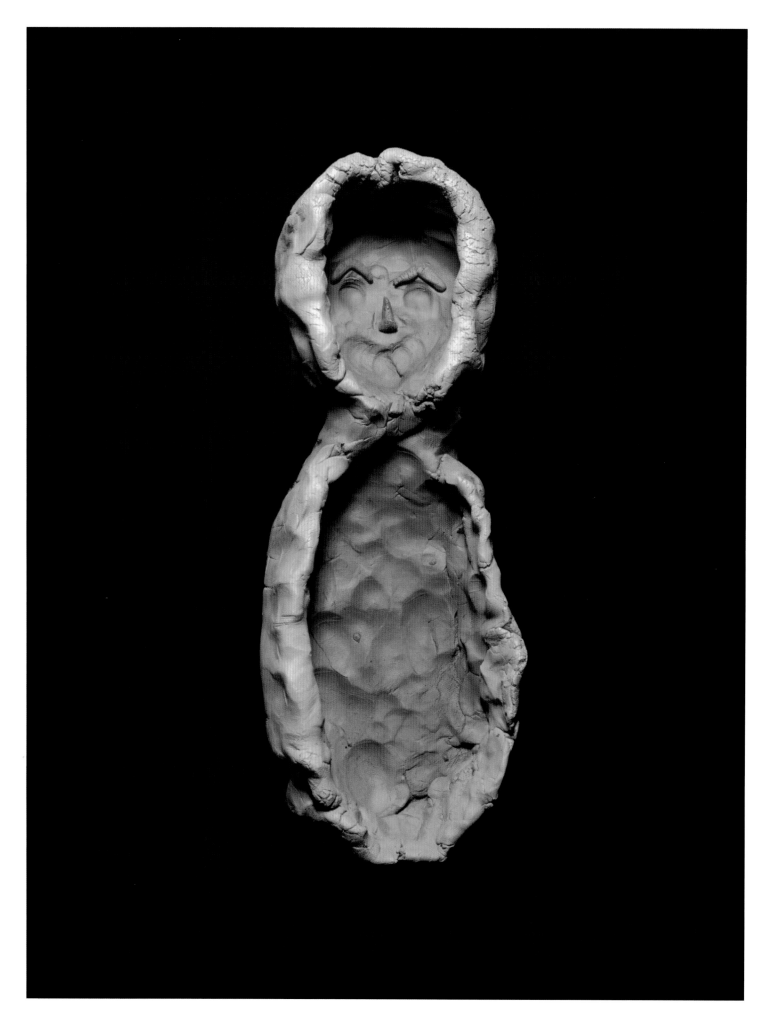

Vessel

Female Protected by Rocks and Tree

The Lucky One

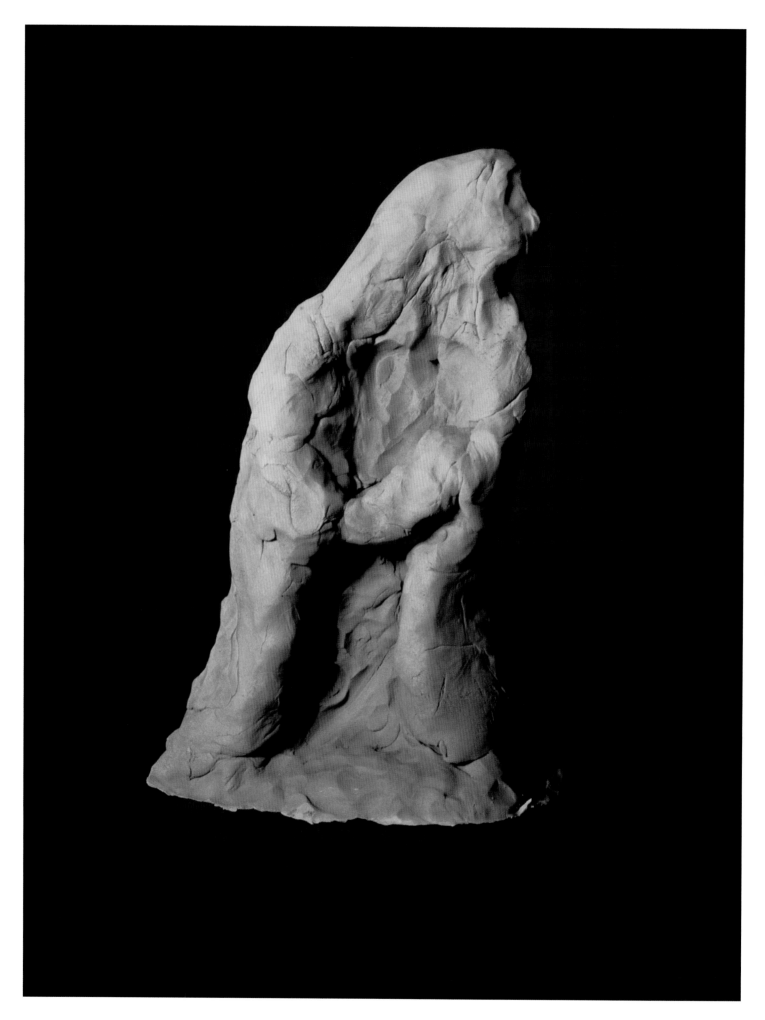

Damsel in Distress

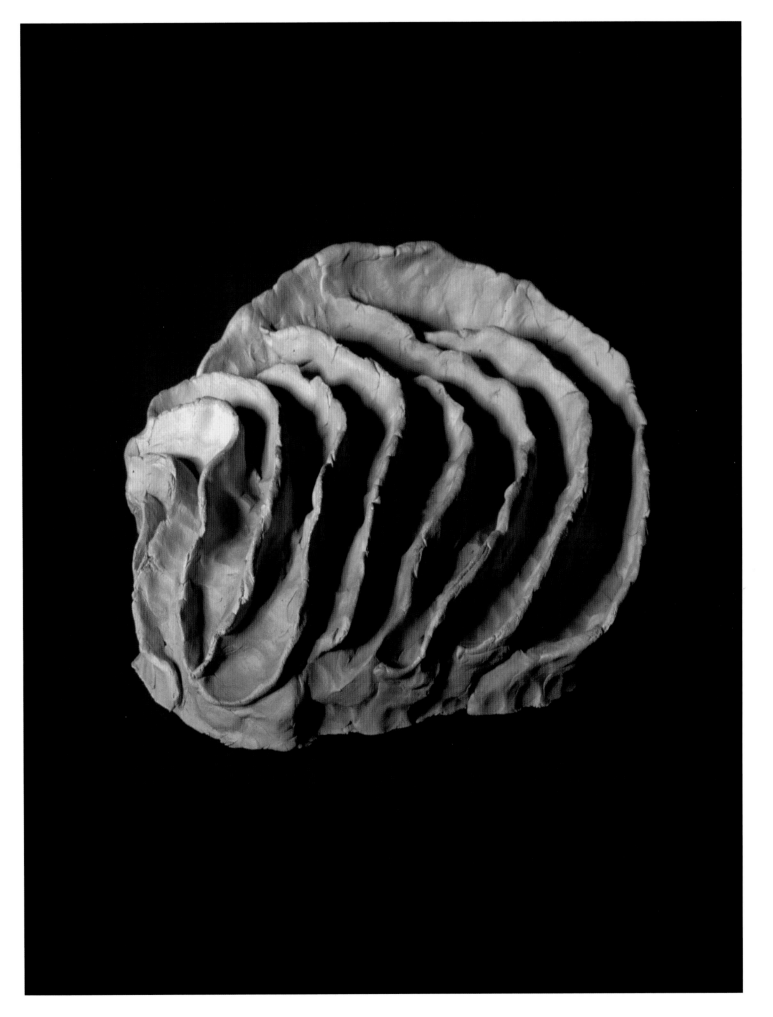

Successive Barriers

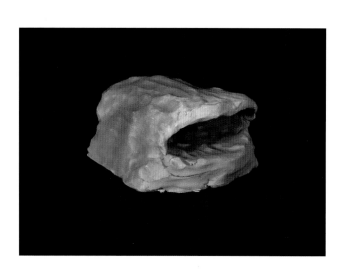

Frog

Small Duck in Big Pond

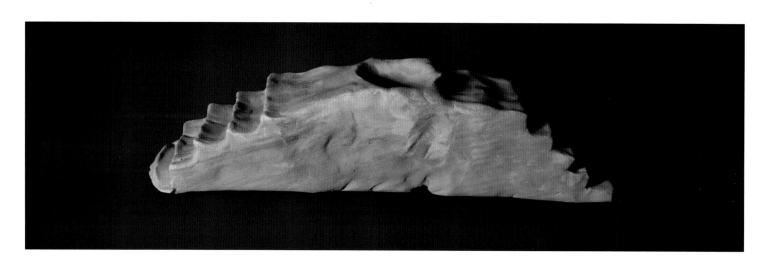

Bridge of Inhibition

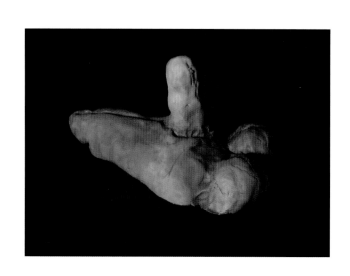

Self-Portrait

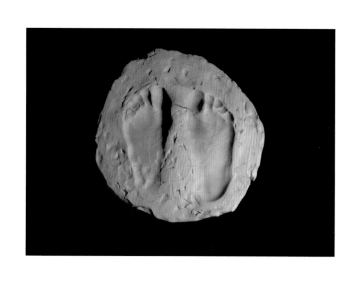

Flat Feet, Off Balance

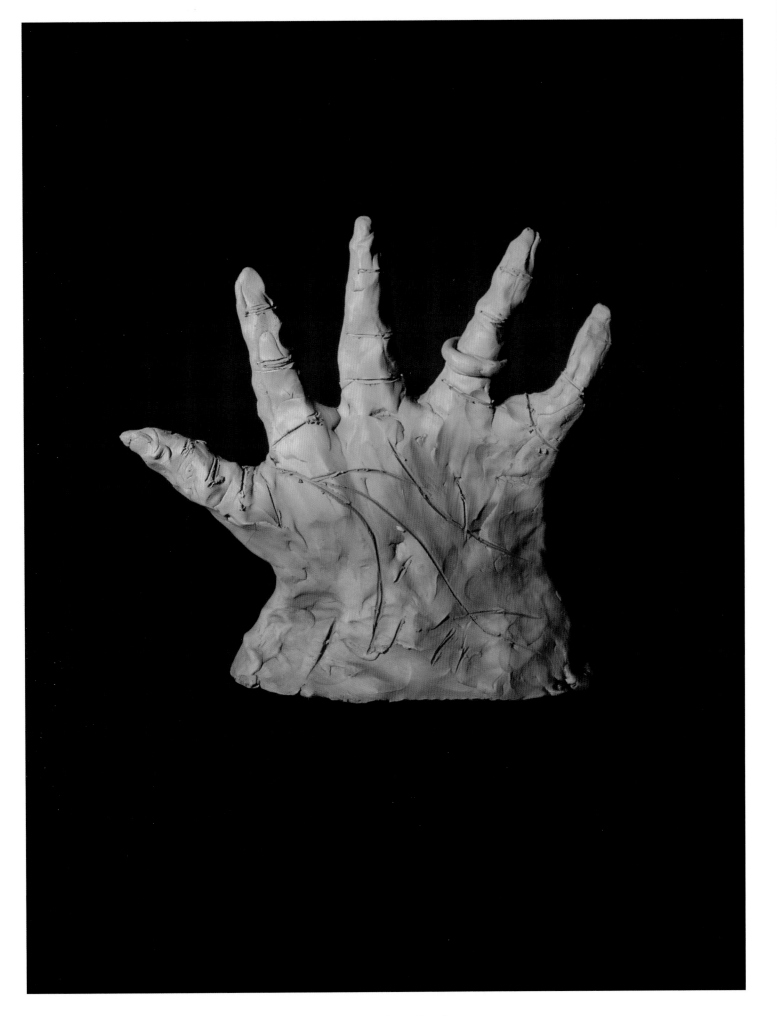

Hardworking Hand

Errant

Ah. Rhythm. Flow.
It's exciting, isn't it?
It's like scat (the musical kind).
And he wrote it so fast.

So what is Valicenti's message, after all? The piece has some rough sections:

_An ironic-to-cynical view of contemporary culture PAGES 86–88
_"I am designer": A rosy view of the power and glory of being a designer PAGES 88–90
_Responsibility shifts (combine section 2 with section 1) to "we" PAGES 91–93
_Questions and second thoughts PAGE 94
_Hostility as purge PAGES 95–96

What are we left with?
Do you think the hubris of section 2 is in fact purged by the contrition/self-questioning of section 4?
Does anyone other than Valicenti come away from the piece with greater clarity or relief?
Does the whole thing seem kind of smug to you — in particular this:
"oops did i say something to disturb you?"
Did you simply enjoy it or did it bug you?

—Sam Potts, critique posted on UnderConsideration.com, September 2003

Dear Emigre,

Congratulations on Issue #64 and the return to dialog-driven content. It is nice to read the thoughts offered by the various authors; the work of Kenneth FitzGerald and Shawn Wolfe is especially strong.

When I saw that Rick Valicenti was a contributor to an issue purporting "…to challenge today's young designers to develop a critical attitude toward their own work and the design scene in general," I looked forward to his perspective, knowing him to be an engaging and insightful man (we had a one-on-one discussion after his presentation in Portland a few years back). Unfortunately, I was left in total confusion as to his motives or intent and instead found *Cranky* to be a pitiful display of arrogance that made me so embarrassed I couldn't finish it. I don't care what Rick believes his stature in American design history to be — *Cranky* is utterly stupid.

Please forgive me for accentuating the negative, but I hold *Emigre* in high regard and hate to see it stoop to such levels because of an author's "stature." Please encourage Rick to read FitzGerald's *Quietude* before his next submission.

—Mike Kippenhan, letter to the editor, *Emigre* 65, September 2003

The Peace Dividend

The critical rehash of the grunge typography debate in *Rant* is peculiar in that almost no one acknowledges his or her involvement in the fracas. Rick Valicenti's rambling mea culpa, *6.26.02: Cranky*, is a glaring exception. It is perhaps the most important article in *Rant* because it suggests a way past the post-traumatic stress disorder that cripples so much contemporary criticism. Valicenti takes credit for all ("I am the embodiment of culture") and admits to all ("We raped the street of its character"). Perhaps what graphic design needs is an opportunity for all sides in the Legibility Wars to come clean, a Truth and Reconciliation Commission of sorts. Then maybe we can move on and begin to examine graphic design as a process that inscribes economic and social context. A dialogue based on the presupposition that design is not only an open creative process but a conversation with the world beyond design may help move our profession in unexpected and reckless directions — a sure sign of growth.

—Dmitri Siegel, "Context in Critique," *Adbusters*, September–October 2003

6.26.02: Cranky

By Rick Valicenti

When I invited Rick Valicenti to contribute to this issue (on June 26, 2002), within hours I received his "rant," which is printed on the following pages. We did caution Rick with a brief missive that said: "Hi Rick. Nothing like a spur of the moment genuine rant! You touch all the bases. If this is really your contribution to No.64, that's allright with me. No problem for me to run as is, set line for line. I should say, just so you know, that it will run alongside other people's 'rants' who will spend months thinking about theirs." Rick wanted me to mention this. RUDY V.

geez

it's 4:30 am
and I'm typing to Rudy V
(what the fuck is wrong with this picture?)

Martha Stewart's stock price has dropped 37%
insider trading secrets bubble to the surface

ohmigod
what if Martha goes to jail!

yikes

is that worse than Winona goin' to jail?

let's not talk about it now

there's fires in Arizona
the world is coming to an end
love lost fires still rage in Colorado
lil' girls kidnapped in just 'bout every town
other intern's bones found in the park

please, God, I hope we never lose Martha
we love Martha

she is our modern vestal virgin

she made style a good thing
she made simplicity feel right again
she made MFA clean typography from Yale
mean something
she makes holidays a joy
she captured our spirit for living

thank you, thank you

I read recently that 6 of 10 Americans are obese
actually they are only 20 pounds or more
overweight

whew

I'm 20 pounds overweight
but I never considered myself obese

as I watch my weight
I find myself watching the weight of others.

damn, there's fat facts everywhere!

everyone has a double chin and saddlebags
or at least 6 of 10 citizens do
big time population growth

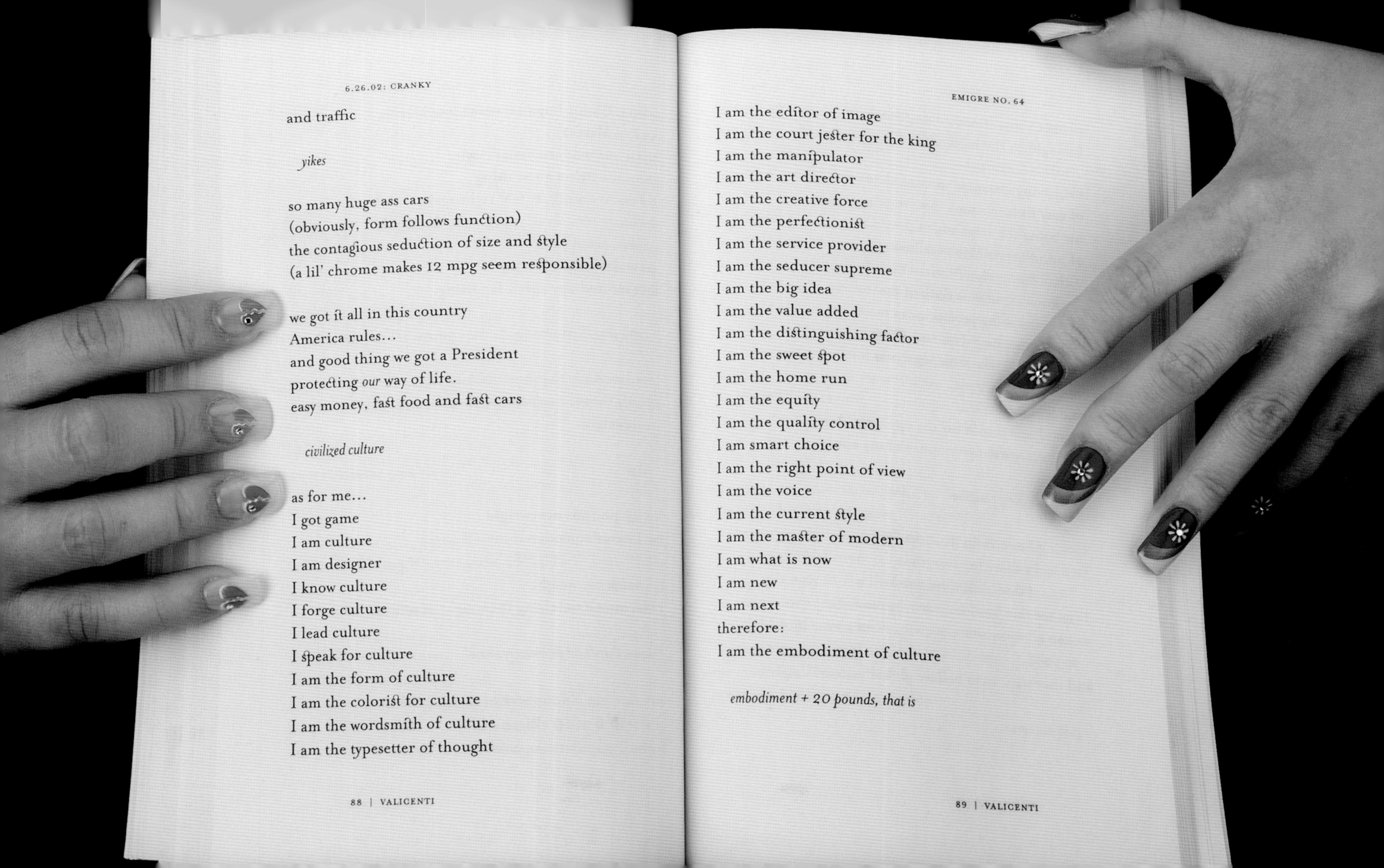

and traffic

yikes

so many huge ass cars
(obviously, form follows function)
the contagious seduction of size and style
(a lil' chrome makes 12 mpg seem responsible)

we got it all in this country
America rules...
and good thing we got a President
protecting *our* way of life.
easy money, fast food and fast cars

civilized culture

as for me...
I got game
I am culture
I am designer
I know culture
I forge culture
I lead culture
I speak for culture
I am the form of culture
I am the colorist for culture
I am the wordsmith of culture
I am the typesetter of thought

I am the editor of image
I am the court jester for the king
I am the manipulator
I am the art director
I am the creative force
I am the perfectionist
I am the service provider
I am the seducer supreme
I am the big idea
I am the value added
I am the distinguishing factor
I am the sweet spot
I am the home run
I am the equity
I am the quality control
I am smart choice
I am the right point of view
I am the voice
I am the current style
I am the master of modern
I am what is now
I am new
I am next
therefore:
I am the embodiment of culture

embodiment + 20 pounds, that is

being in this esteemed position...
I delight in the moment and reward myself
with a fanny pat
for having provided more than my share
of easy fixes to numb our everyday existence,
for being the value added provider
of mindless dribble to sell *more*
than the competition
for knowing what is the best means of
manipulating perceptions.
for all those long daze and all nighters,
oh yes, I did take more than one for our team

and looking back...
I simply say thanks for the opportunities
for it was worth every ounce of my energy

just look at my portfolio

looking down from 30,000 feet
(if I had a dime for everytime
I heard that bullshit phrase)
I can see that hard work has its rewards.
we can all agree western civilization never looked
so good
and they want us to believe globalization is right

glad you agree

in fact, give yourself a fanny pat
you deserve credit too
you are one of us
together, we made everything seem so groovy

you know...
we made logos a real necessity
we made the swoosh ubiquitous
we made branding the holy grail
we made communication a number one concern
we made modernism mod
we made post modernism go away
we made the grunge an aesthetic
we made the internet

sorry, Al

we made the interfaces flash
we made banner ads, too!
we made up the idea of spam
we made annual reports
society's easy to read/must read bible
we made corporate leaders into rock stars
we put the spin in motion
we made success attainable in our lifetime
we made it all look so easy
we made it all seem so valuable

oh yeah, along the way...
we succumbed to the obligatory focus group testing

will sacrifice evenings for catered cold cuts and cheddar cubes

we digitally enhanced the naughty bits and zits
we dabbled gratuitously in support of sustainability
we provided big time lip service
    on behalf of commerce
we held the sweaty palms of big business
we spelled risk in lower case type
we made fonts popular for everyone
we provided choices to pick from
we created the illusion of customization
we replaced content with messaging
we thought information equaled inspiration
we turned our back on meaning
we stumbled to author real content
we formatted everything
we distilled experience while touting its virtues
we digested all thoughts prior to spitting them back
we fabricated truths when there were only lies
we hypnotized our public with illusion
we raped the street of its character
we appropriated the counter culture
we commodified the artists
we became the great producers
    for not so great product
we felled the forests for advertising's inserts

we covered every surface with die-cut vinyl noise
we silenced the naysayers across the conference
    tables with blah blah blah
we did what we were told whenever necessary
we earned graduate degrees to measure up
we learned to speak in power point
we labeled ourselves in black
we flaunted client lists like badges of honor
we turned some of our own into culture's gods
we let Chairman Mau define life style
we tried to be important
and on our path we rarely said...

no.

so what do we have to show for all our overtime?
quite a bit actually,
while consumed by the sweet smell of success...
we produced glossy zines showcasing our bounty
    and sweat
we partied mindlessly hard at our national
    conferences
we hid behind well-meaning manifestos
we idolized our own
we became the shit that didn't smell

'cause we made everything groovy

Now that's the stuff we can all sign our name to

success has its rewards
take no prisoners
ride into the sunset
be all you can be
get to know no boundaries
dive into your pleasure
invest so you can retire
elevate your game

damn

gotta go to a meeting and I'm late
be certain the revisions get out right away
and, wouldya make that call for me?
could ya also do this
and do that
do this
do that
do this
do that
do this
do that

please?

~~fuck~~ you
just do it
ah...
~~fuck~~ this

6.26.02: CRANKY

so kick back...
make yourself comfy and ask:
what (the ~~fuck~~) did we really do during our
    professional lives?
what did we do with all those award certificates?
what right answers have we really provided?
what serious problems did we really solve as
    problem solvers?
what difference did we really make?
what wisdom have we really left behind?
what have we really said about ourselves?
what do we make that we can really be proud of?
what have we done to show we really care?
what of our (collective) offering really feels
    enlightened?
what messages have we spread to really insure a
    peaceful spirit?
what goods and services have we aligned ourselves
    with that are good services?
what might our soul really look like?
what image in the mirror should we really believe?

oops, did I say something to disturb you?

well, we all know:
('cause we told each other and the world through
    the messages we craft)
life's short, play hard
win at all costs

f*ck that
no...
f*ck you
no...
f*ck yourself
what da f*ck did you say?
f*ck you
no, f*ck you, asshole!
take this
take that
eat me

what?
you heard me
f*ck you
f*ck off you fat f*ck

ah, f*ck it.

now dontcha feel a little bit better?

6:53 am

(I type with only two fingers)

It's time to get serious. There is an issue that demands the concerted energies of all designers. Each of us must promise *real* human presence within each artifact of communication we design. Every so often we emerge from our trancelike state, murmuring our beloved mantra — pro-duc-tion-val-ues — only to discover that the sediment has hardened on top of our feet of clay. As a profession, we all recite the script and we all fondle the same tools. Our fees are fixed and the codes are known both by us and by our ultimate audiences. But at this very moment, because of our tired and repetitive communications conventions, some very dangerous assumptions about "content" are being cherished. While we can use numbers to justify the use of such tried-and-true solutions, we are running a risk that our efforts at communication may be ignored. In the past, we have seen design snap out of its zone. In the mid-1970s, as the profession was earning its stripes in the business sector, armed with a targeted, easy-to-use version of modernism, the underground was responding in a not-so-nice fashion. With safety pins through the cheek came the torn edges of a ransom note and the drip of blood on paper. The punk movement spawned a new language of form and a new code. Human presence was reborn *on the surface.*

Professionals appropriated the new code until it, too, stopped making real contact, for essence does not live on the surface. Now everyone on the receiving end of our communications knows exactly how to respond to subtly mutating lures. The "strategically" designed and commodified din we spew will ultimately interfere with meaningful reception. Something fundamental is lost in design's translation: why does it feel like no one is really present in most professionally designed communications? Long ago, *form* was lowered from its canonical position when it faltered in service to the design's functionality. *Interactivity* was moved into the hallowed niche but has since been condensed and reduced to a sidebar. So I ask you: *what is missing?* Real Human Presence. Affecting the surface alone doesn't affect anyone. Instead, as communicators, we need to ask how we can design compelling, truthful evidence of human exchange. We, the first generation of designers to be respected by business and armed with tools of unprecedented power, must challenge stale professional conventions and reawaken the essence of our humanity in all of our communications. Civilization will forever be served when we find what we have forgotten we have lost: our reason for being. We must serve, honor, and respect human presence by design! RV_04.01.2001

The Herman Miller Showroom Digital Petroglyph Film

While "Mid-Life Executives: *Lost* works in clay" is a peculiar artifact of an unusually revealing session, the sculptures form hard evidence that contemporary humanity longs to make real contact with itself.

We find ourselves asking this type of question. How can communications design evidence human touch without relying on the conventions of gestural brush strokes, collage, and quote marks?

There is no single answer, no answer "for all time." Even a technique that is heart-catchingly fresh at first sight looks hollow after its thousandth uninspired use. Intrigue eludes.

Here's one of a few clues we have found.

Digital Petroglyph — a fifty-four-minute digital film conceived and directed for Herman Miller's 1999 Neocon showroom — is a realized response to the problem of locating human presence in communications design. Motion-mapped code was the foundation for all of the decision-making related to action, movement, color blends, etc. Digital Petroglyph began with a question and a hypothesis.

What is it that immediately distinguishes real human motion from mathematical animation?

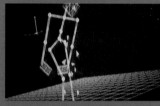

Perhaps it's the mistakes: the twitches and hitches of muscle groups contradicting each other at any of millions of moments every day to hesitate, doubt, observe, rethink, refocus, giggle, remember, regret. Human beings make their way beautifully through the world, but not smoothly.

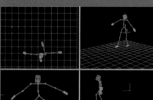

Maybe that is why movie heroes are so appealing — the actors are in no real danger in a dangerous scene. Their well-rehearsed motions are smooth and relaxed and untroubled by decision in a way ours never are in real life.

We wired two dancers with thirteen sensors apiece and asked them to physically express and respond to words aligned with "stability" and "agility," the key message vocabulary of the client. We recorded their motion digitally, in three dimensions. They danced, they climbed, they performed everyday actions. But the moments that really caught our attention — the moments we played over and over for our own pleasure while we changed the motion map to display stick figures, then biomorphic blobs, and finally pure geometries — were the moments between "takes," moments when the dancers were simply standing, making tiny movements, unconsciously stretching, listening to direction, talking to each other. These motions were so natural, so recognizable, so vulnerable, so undeniably human, that it didn't matter what graphic form was chosen to express them — even the cubes and planes had personality! At last, we had electronic motion that equaled e-motion.

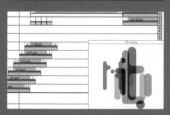

Digital Petroglyph was born.

As we edited, we worked those moments of silliness or jitters or vulnerability into the fabric of the film. The result was a particular realism. We chuckled to see those raw moments drawing eyes and turning heads as we observed the crowd at the opening.

DIGITAL PETROGLYPH_ PYLON DESIGN INSTALLED IN SHOWROOM_1999

DIGITAL PETROGLYPH_200 OF THE 77,760 FRAMES_1999

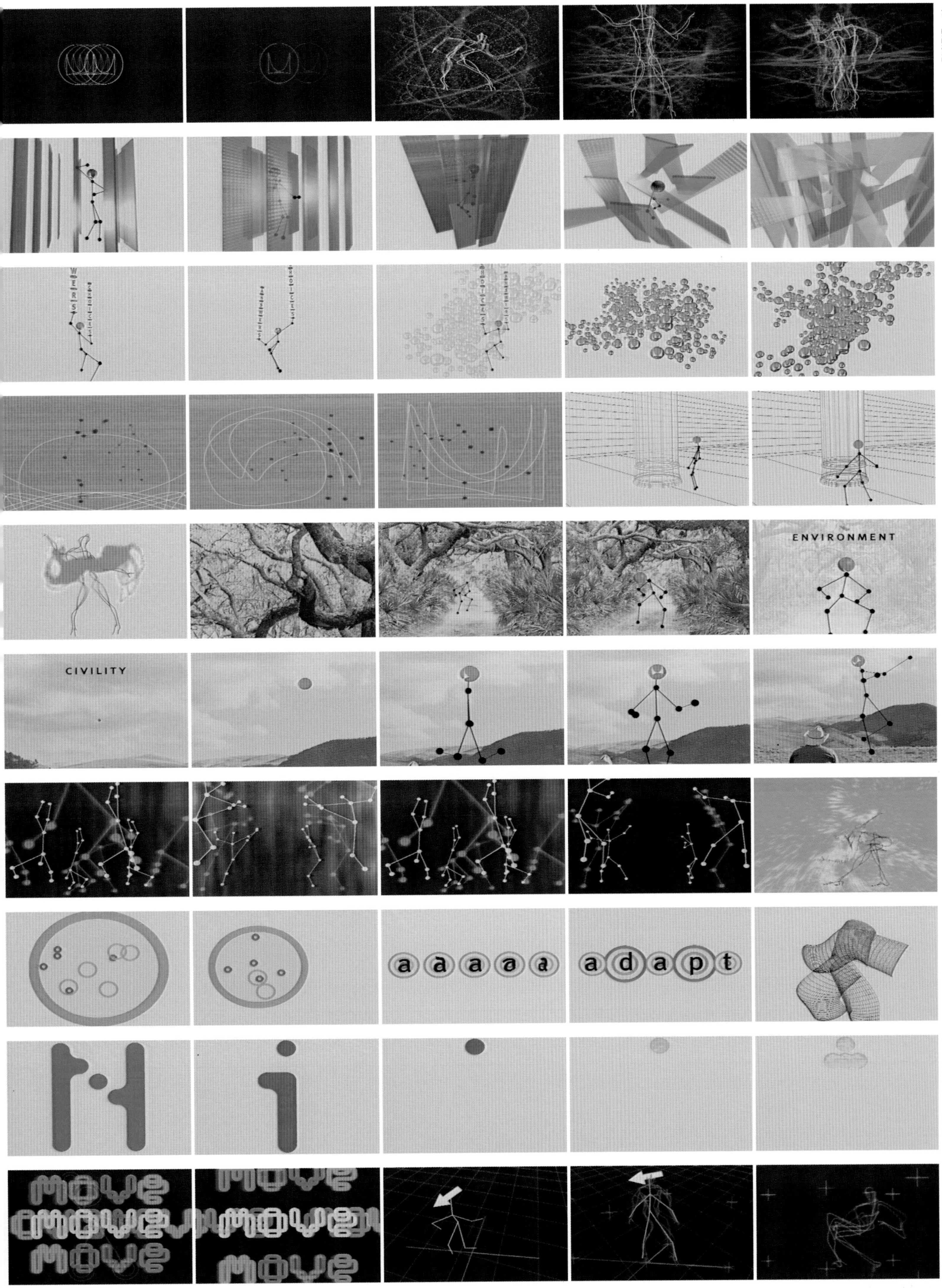
ENVIRONMENT
CIVILITY
a a a a a
adapt
move
move
move

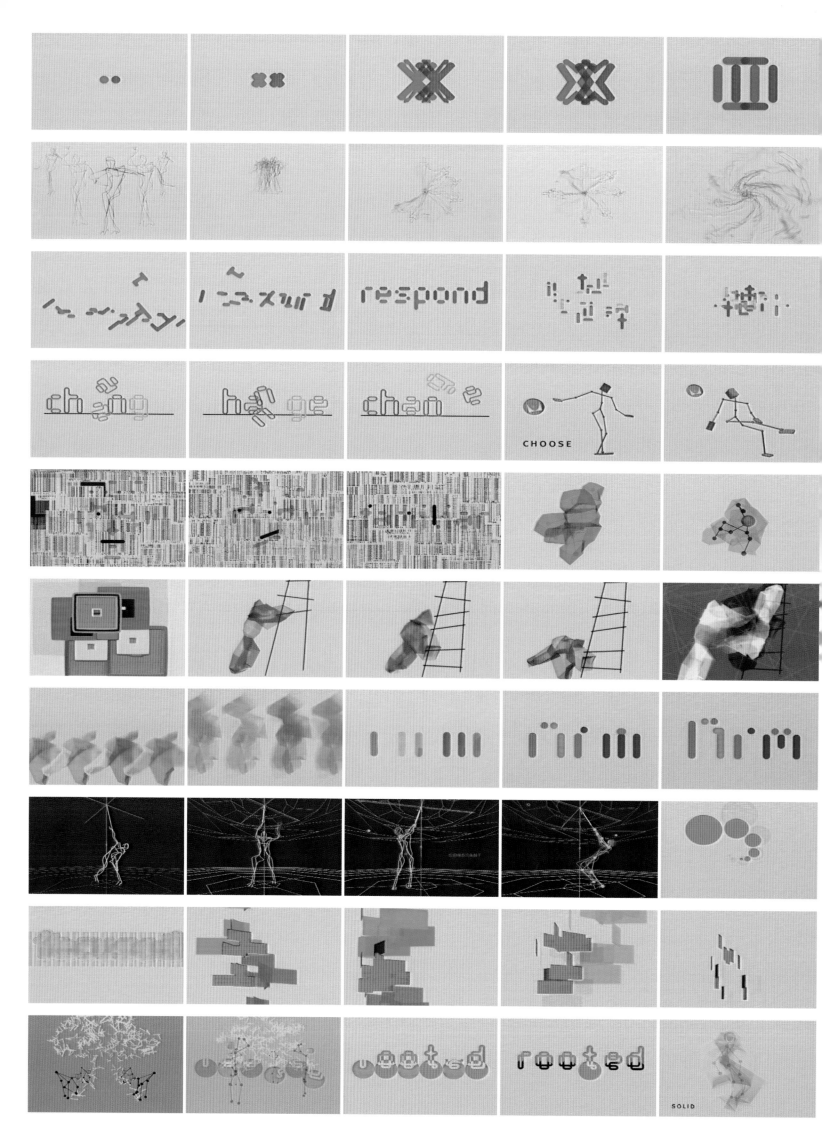

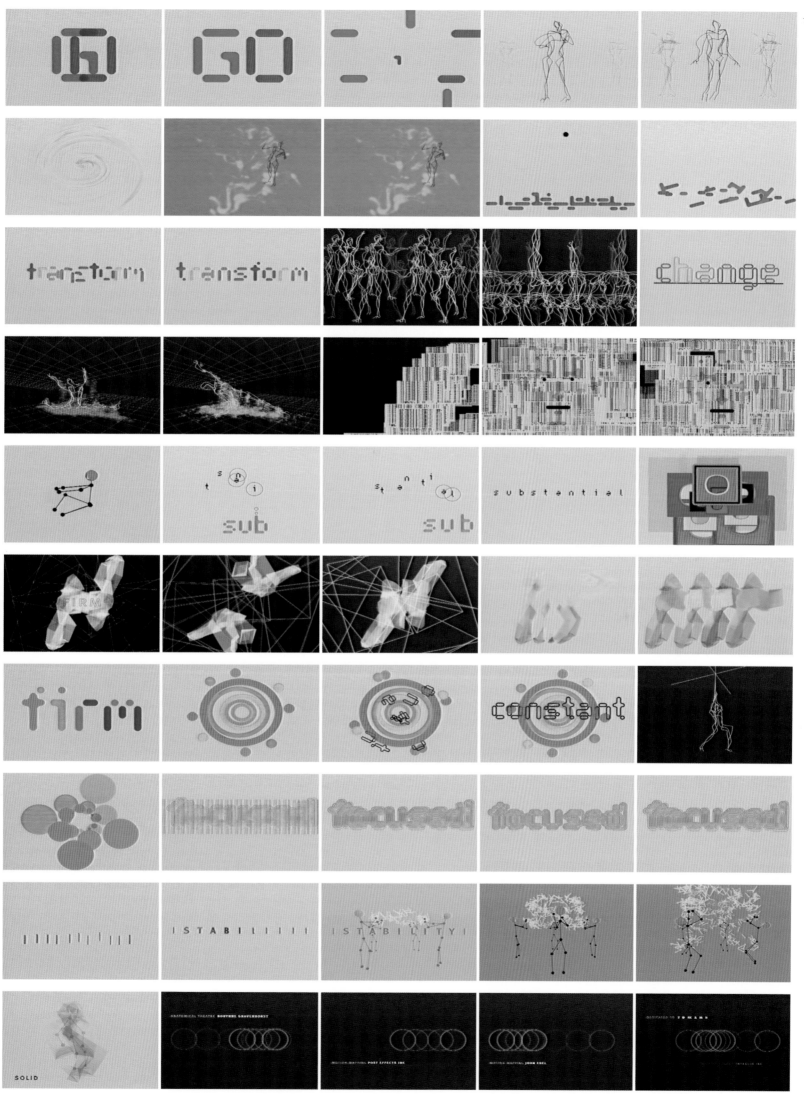

CREDITS: CONCEIVED AND DIRECTED BY RV; VISUALIZED IN 3-D BY MATT DALY; EDITED AND COMPOSITED BY VELLO VIRKHAUS; TYPOGRAPHIC ANIMATION BY GB; OPENING SEQUENCE INSPIRED BY "POWERS OF TEN" BY CHARLES AND RAY EAMES

Digital Reflecting Pool

At Herman Miller's West Michigan Greenhouse reception area, visitors interact with a twenty-eight-by-four-foot piece of steel floating twenty inches off the floor. Two twenty-eight-foot-by-eighteen-inch benches line the sides. Along the benches rise eight hand-poured glass forms that beg to be touched.

When a glass receptor is touched, it activates a digital reflecting pool of designed imagery. The patterns respond like water, fluidly propagating in real time over the full length of the surface. They are undisturbed until the actions at one sensor begin to mesh with ripples set in motion at another receptor. The waves of energy travel seamlessly through five ceiling-mounted projectors.

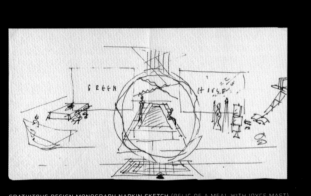

GRATUITOUS DESIGN MONOGRAPH NAPKIN SKETCH (RELIC OF A MEAL WITH JOYCE MAST)
GOOD IDEAS OFTEN HAPPEN OVER FOOD, WHICH IS WHY NAPKINS ARE MADE OF PAPER

The Digital Reflecting Pool applies an organic motion to a nearly infinite variety of images, patterns, or texts. There, at the edge of a digital river, throwing stones, visitors can watch the current go by, experiencing Herman Miller's leadership in manufacturing and service responsiveness. Experience is the message and the message is experience.

Sometimes human presence is made manifest by a magic trick — causing obviously natural phenomena to take place in obviously artificial settings. What's shared is both the subtlety of observation and the skill of imitation. The resulting moment of disbelief — the wow moment — is the human contact. It's a wink from designer to audience.

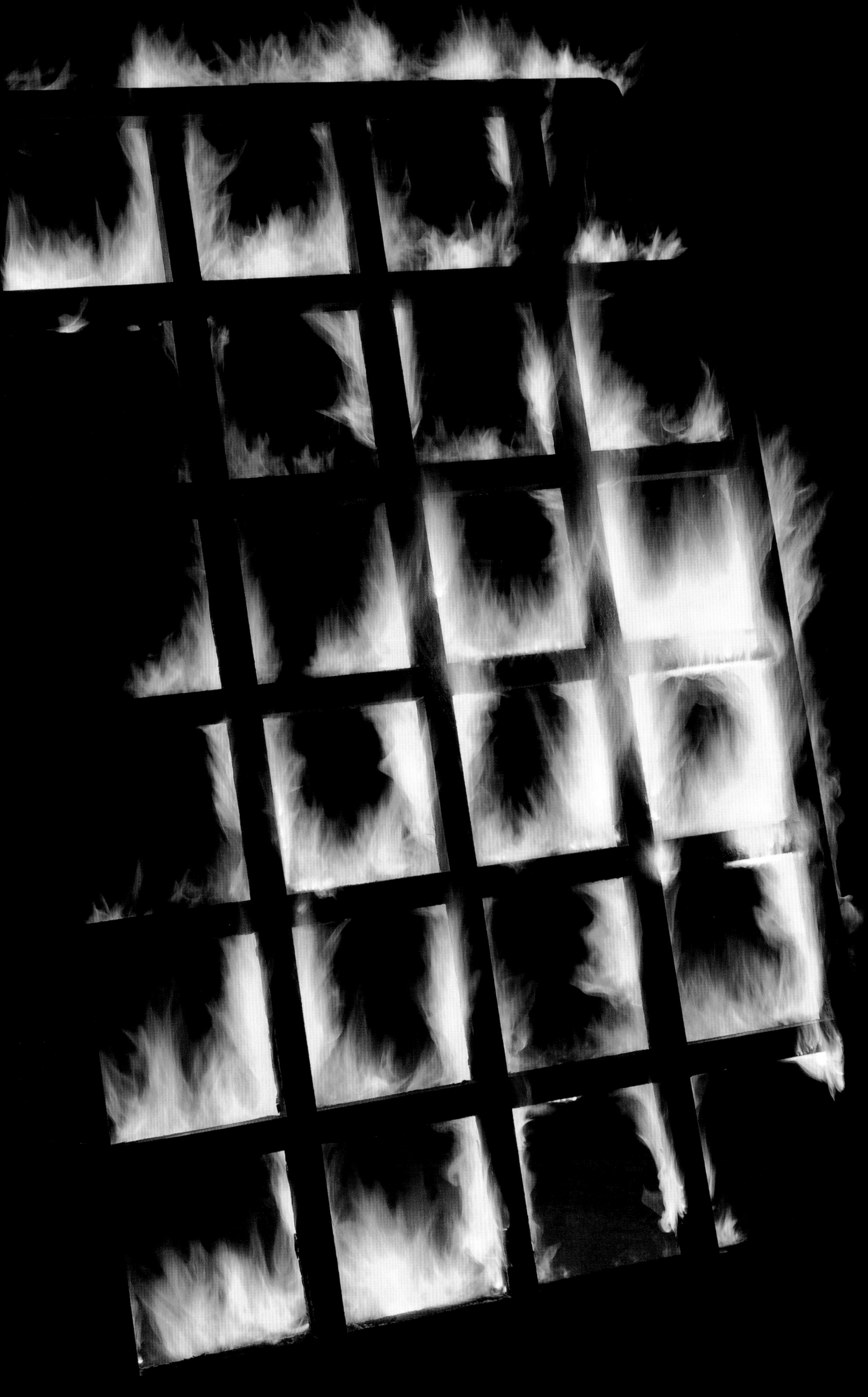

G

I LOVE

GILBERT

PAPER

1988　1989　1990　1991　1992　1993　1994　1995　1996　1997　1998　1999　2000　2001　2002　2003

Shirley Jean Frick

Su McLoughlin

Kathy Merckx

GETTING REACQUAINTED

Hi, Kathy. This is Shirley…

Oh, my God!

How are you?

I'm fine.

Hi.

I recognize that voice.

This is Su.

Hi, Su. This is Shirley Jean.

And Kathy Merckx here.

Hi, Merckxy!

Oh, this is great. And you're still here in the Valley?

Yes, I am.

And I never, ever, ever, ever run into you. I can't believe it.

I know!

Wow.

We've got ten years of catching up to do. This could be a while.

laughs

Wow. laughs

I was there. I was there at Rick's first presentation to Gilbert.
Yes, that was a proud moment.

Here we were, sort of the uptight, corporate, you know, marketing staff in Gilbert Paper in Menasha. We thought we were doing a pretty darn good job with all of our design projects through the years. In one fell swoop, as I recall, he — Rick — basically took not only Gilbert's design, but the whole paper industry's design, and literally put it in a wastebasket that had been placed on our conference table, and told us that that's what most designers do with paper projects when they get them.

We were just sort of blown away, and we didn't know quite what to make of it. But what he said made a lot of sense to us. And that's partly why he got the job.

Were you there, Su?   I was also there.   Okay.

And I recall it as Shirley Jean does. But also, I recall Rick giving us a story of, basically, "You're asking me to endorse your product. And why would I want to endorse your product?" And he captivated the audience because, as Shirley Jean said, we were pretty conservative. And Rick, in his infinite wisdom, passed around some messages that weren't e-mails at that time. They were mostly voice messages and faxes that had come into his office about how great Thirst work was. And so they were passed out to everyone in attendance.

And I remember the feeling after he had captivated us — we had already met with a couple of other designers. We had a short list, and Rick was the last one to come in. And after he left, we all wanted to assess him, and he had moved each one of us to the point where we wanted to leave the meeting and go right to his studio.

Which I think we did, didn't we?

Yes, we did.

It was within roughly an hour's time. We were back on the phone with him and then we said, "Can we hear more? Can we see more? Can we see what you're all about?" Because he was so refreshing

We met — I think he was scurrying to get his office cleaned up. The whole studio, I think, was probably flabbergasted that we had called. He and his sister, Barbara, were there. We met with her. I think they gave us a tour. Do you remember much more, Su?

I remember the tour of the office, specifically the fabric ceiling in the bathroom.

Oh, really. And the Wrigley chair?

Right.

But I recall it as you do, Shirley Jean. I mean, they scrambled and got everything ready. And I think Rick realized that an impact had been made.

We couldn't get him out of our heads. We all had different reasons for being moved. But it was obvious that we were all moved by him.

Yes, and not just Su and me, but Pat Robinson, the president of Gilbert at that time, and the VP of marketing. And these are people that, I think, generally don't get moved very much. But I think they were as well.

THE "WASTEBASKET MEETING"

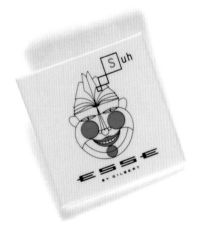

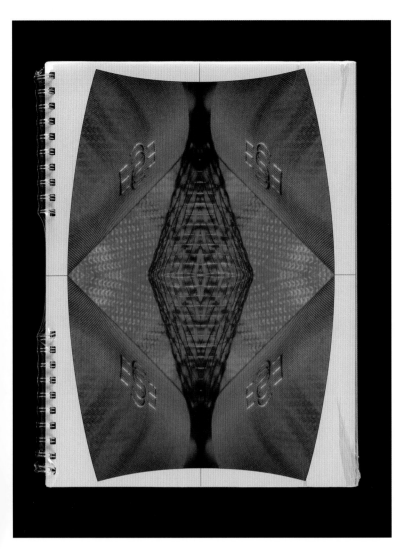

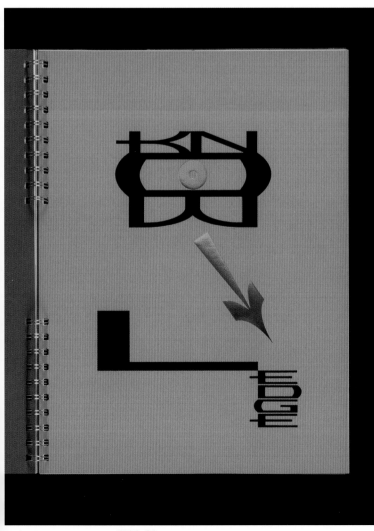

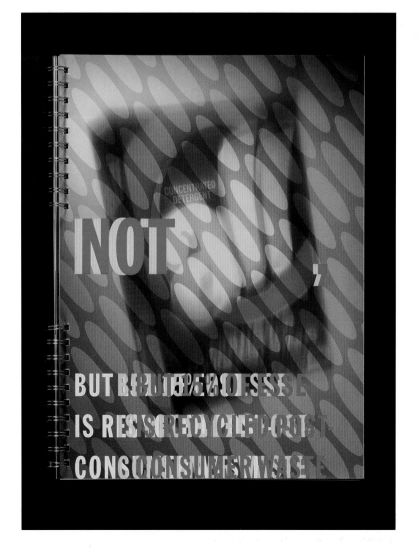

INTRODUCTORY ESSE PROMOTION_1989-90

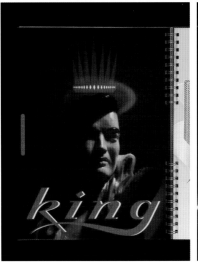
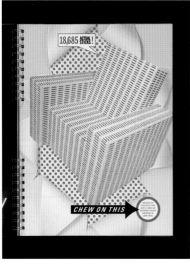

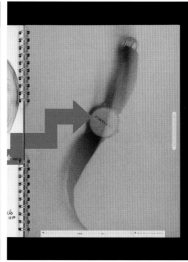

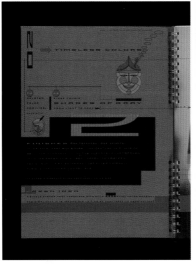

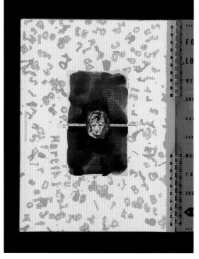
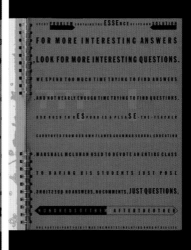

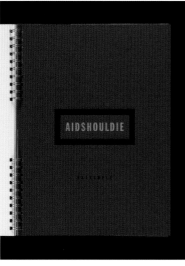
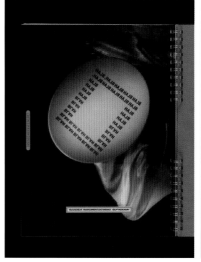
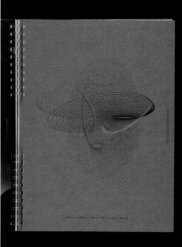

THE ESSE BOOK

Shirley Jean started with the Esse project. It was a new beginning — basically a new beginning for the company. And then I came in, and it was in the growth of the paper grade, and then Kathy has been there in recent years during the product's maturity.

I was in more of the production role, and so I didn't always work directly with Rick. I worked with Michael Giammanco on the big Esse book. So I wasn't in that meeting, or any of the initial conceptions. But then, once it became production — which, by the way, Rick, in his ever-soaring quest for excitement, had, what, thirty-some printers, or twenty — what the heck was it? Twenty-nine printers I think it was, each one doing a different page. And it was Michael G's and my job to coordinate all those printers.

Then Su, you would start to say, "Kath, this is your job. Now you call Rick." I'd say, "No, no. I can't call Rick! Oh, my God."

That was a *cluster.* But boy, I tell you, it was a great training ground. And so I was always more involved with the production people, and had rare contact with Rick for the first couple of years.

Right…

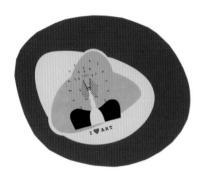

And I sat on the phone, and I had to push him, you know, I don't like this, I like this, I think we should do this. And I was dying, because I didn't want to have to push back to a designer to say, I don't like your design. Because who am I to say I don't like your design? And now I do it weekly. *laughs* I have no problem calling Rick now and telling him I don't like that.

He always says I'm his check and balance, because I'm pretty much a realist, and obviously, I have no design background, so I look at things much more practically than he ever did, I guess. And so I sort of bring that level to it.

We just went through this three or four days ago, and we're starting this new piece, introducing a new offering. And we spent probably three hours on the phone. And we go back and forth and then it'll get to a point where I'm like, "Rick, I can't even think anymore. I need to just go to bed for the night and call back tomorrow and start over."

And the next day, within an hour and a half, we have the solution. And now he'll go forward with design, and then we'll discuss it back and forth.

Rick is incredibly creative and will take it as far as you allow him to take it. So he always usually goes way out, and then I've got to kind of pull him back a little bit.

For me, on the Esse book, I learned early on that, in order for it to be successful, I would have to give up any fear that I might have and become trusting. And once I overcame the fear and passed on the trust, then I felt very comfortable with the situation. I actually — for me, I wanted to get inside Rick's head all the time, to understand what he was thinking, and then bring it into the application for the business.

And I think, from what Kathy was saying, these days Kathy already has the concept of where she wants it to be for the business. So, you know, we worked a little bit differently. But I felt that there was a level of friction that we needed to experience in order for the project to be successful.

The way we debuted the book in Chicago, I think, was interesting, too. Joyce Picalla was the specification rep in the Chicago market for us, and she helped us debut this in that market, with a party — a coming-out party — at Oprah's studio.

Well, and then we repeated it in New York and L.A., didn't we?

Yes. In Chicago it was a fairly big splash. And you know, just to put our product on the same sort of name recognition as, say, an Oprah, for example, just by the venues that we chose, I think, really said a lot to the design community.

ESSE BOOK DEBUT EVENTS

But definitely, the Chicago one was the most spectacular, because it was Rick's hometown. We knew that all of his peers would turn out. It was an unbelievable event.

Then the tour extended to Australia. See, I actually traveled first to Australia and New Zealand with slides — Rick's slides — and spoke to groups in five different cities in Australia, and then also New Zealand. And then subsequently, after I had left, Rick actually went on tour in Australia.

Wow.

Yeah.

Jeff Miller went with him.
Yeah.

All on Esse?

At that time it had expanded beyond Esse, because then Rick started doing everything. And so it was more about Gilbert as a whole.

What was the initial response on the Esse book — I know from the design community it was awesome and incredible — but was there any pushback from the sales force or the merchants, from printers?

SUPPORT FOR THE ESSE BOOK FROM THE EXECUTIVE VP

The one situation that I remember so very clearly in my mind — and it's hard if people don't really know the players — is that the pretty conservative executive VP received the piece and studied it over the weekend and came in and described it to the sales group. And he really found things in it that I don't think anyone ever expected would have come from his mouth. His transformation into accepting a piece as wild as that was enough to persuade everyone at Gilbert that, ultimately, this was the right thing.

I think as pieces went on and on, and they became either a little bit edgy or similar, then, of course, everybody had their own opinion.

YOUR IDENTITY HERE

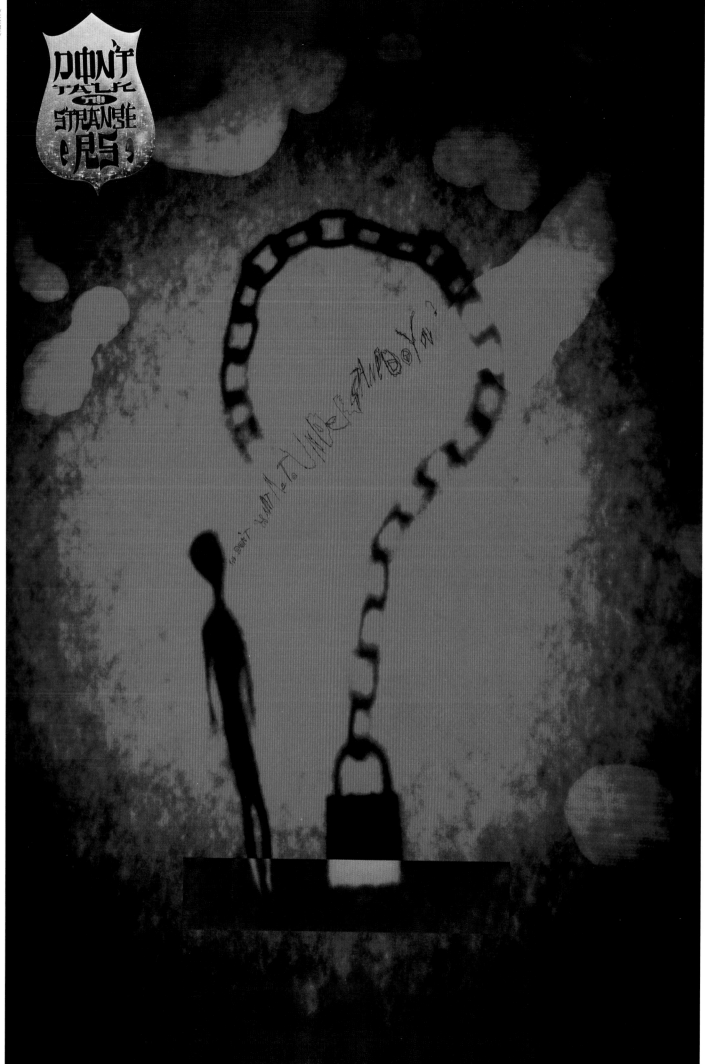

DON'T TALK TO STRANGERS_ LECTURE ANNOUNCEMENT POSTER _1995

You know, I remember probably three or four years ago, we were getting a lot of heat from the sales force that everything was Rick, everything was Rick, and it all looks the same, and it's all over-designed, and it's all — you know, that whole thing.

And we had a very intense meeting — I call it the come-to-Jesus meeting. I mean, it was a tough meeting. And we just said, here's a list of the things that we believe you bring to us, and here's some of the pushback we're getting. And the list of what he brought was very lengthy. He's a strategic thinker besides being a designer. He's got a business head, and yet he can turn around and take whatever you just said and put it into visuals. In a meeting he's drawing away and all of a sudden he's got this whole concept. But in this big meeting we said to him, "We have got to introduce other designers and other art, and we have to bring some other blood into this. But yet, you are a very important part of this."

And so we sat down and we figured out a way that Rick could almost become sort of the brand keeper, design keeper, if you will. And we brought in a couple of other designers. For example, when we introduced Realm, Rick pointed us to a group of designers, including John Maeda, who was at the time up and coming, and today is this incredible designer who's very well respected in the industry — and Rick named the grade and produced that piece. And so he helped mold it and keep it in focus, and keep it feeling like a Gilbert piece incorporating somebody else's art. And at first we thought, oh man, you know, these designers are going to say, "Screw this. We're not going to have Rick Valicenti critiquing our work!" When we meet with them the first time, and it is Rick and John Maeda, for example, and myself, it becomes very clear very quickly that Rick is not going to discuss with you what type font you use or what colors you use. He's not here to critique your design. He's here for the whole strategy, the whole conceptual side of it. And it has worked out incredibly well.

Good.

What he shared, really, the same thing that we did in working with him, is that he could give trust to whomever…

Exactly.

…he selected, and also is very generous to have done that because it brings other people into focus. It takes a really strong person…

Yeah.

…to be able to share that generosity.

THE "COME-TO-JESUS MEETING": FRIENDS OF GILBERT

REALM™ IMAGINE THE POSSIBILITIES

And I think that was the evolution of where we stand with our marketing strategy today, the whole bit where we're incorporating other people's artwork. So it's not all about Rick's look or Rick's design. But yet, Rick is an integral part of every bit of it. And then, you also see the talent where Thirst designed all of our swatch books. There's no way you would see those as Rick — you know what I mean? He can mold to whatever he needs to be. He can make it very utilitarian, and he can make it very beautiful and inspiring.

Great.

2404 1992

NEVILLE BRODY/MALCOLM GARRETT/KATHERINE McCOY

PAPER

CHOICE

RICK VALICENTI/KATHERINE McCOY

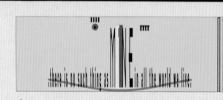

RICK rickvalicenti RICK + KATHERINE

The word Thirst signifies both the name and the impassioned creative drive behind a small studio founded in Chicago by Rick Valicenti in 1988. Champions of a deeply personal approach to graphic design, Valicenti and his collaborator Michael Giammanco have provoked the design establishment with artistic, cheeky experiments that have quickly proven to be a legitimate contribution to design's discourse. Before long, gestures that were used expressively (or ironically) in the Thirst vocabulary made their way into a rash of portfolios, where their witticisms have been largely misinterpreted. Thirst, however, wasn't standing still. When we caught up with Valicenti at O'Hare International airport, he was keen to discuss cake decoration, Attitude Design, and the inspiration behind the Exquisite Corpse experiment you have before you. How has Thirst forged its distinctive, audacious style in the middle of heartland America? The only way I can answer that is to say we're just being ourselves. I'm just being me. And that's not said out of arrogance or false pride — it's just all I know. Not being trained as a graphic designer, I've had to learn how to absolutely trust my instincts. What's your impression about the state of graphic design today? A lot of the #@)% I see out there is so jive ... Well, don't print that. Let's just say a lot of design is derivative, and at this point a lot of it has become derivative of itself, so it's a self-perpetuating spiral. I've become so bored with attitude. I'd rather be on the sideline calling a spade a spade. But you're not on the sideline! At this year's AIGA conference you were at the top of the roster ... Yes, but I'm only servicing a small group of design-driven clients. So in that sense I'm not in a position where I'm supposed to appeal to the mass-market. There's a great deal of freedom in remaining small and running a lean organization. Do the Thirst imitators drag you down? They are of little concern except when they have a negative impact on my business development efforts. In any case if someone copies my typographic gestures, they may not be adopting the reasons for employing those gestures. So how do you stay ahead of the pack? The only way is through provocation. By revealing levels of thinking that are much more in-depth than anything anyone had expected. People are looking for the cake decoration and they aren't going to find it. As I see it, the trap for a designer gets set when he or she starts doing work to fulfill someone else's expectations. Then the designer become static. Thank you very much! That's the story exactly. The primary challenge is to fulfill only your own expectations; for me that often includes poking some fun — even at myself. What was your inspiration for this Exquisite Corpse project? What I told Michael, my partner, was that this project was like tribes sending smoke signals out to each other. We're saying, hey, we're having some fun over here, what's going on over there? And the part that's so exciting to me is to think that designers who respect one another can relinquish their own work to one of their peers, and then embrace someone else's work. What was the smoke signal you sent out? It's a simple thing, partly a self-portrait in type, created from a line from Buddha: THERE IS NO SUCH THING AS MINE IN ALL THE WORLD. To me this quote represented what we are doing, because here I was creating a design on a disk that I'm passing along to Katherine, who will make her mark, and then send it on to Neville, who will transform it again. I wanted to make a statement that what I was sending out was not mine, and the next person should feel free to do with it as they please. To me it's an exhilarating and unnerving way to exchange a message. All egos are checked at the door on this project? Absolutely. Everyone has said nothing is theirs. Helvetica or Franklin Gothic don't belong to any one designer; the use of warm red and black doesn't belong to any one dogma; and the use of arrows doesn't belong to the vernacular. It's all out there for us to use as communication. That is the spirit of this whole project. What do you hope will come of this Exquisite Corpse experiment? My feeling is that if seven designers can work together on this level, then there's no reason why those seven can't join up with seven others and so on. My most optimistic goal is for the world of electronic communication to be made a bit smaller, and for design collaboration to become a bit wider as a result of this global network.

RICK + KATHERINE + NEVILLE

MICHELE DE LUCCHI/TAKENOBU IGARASHI/MILTON GLASER

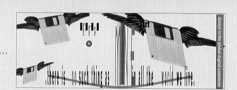

ERIK SPIEKERMANN/PAUL SYCH/ARMAND MEVIS AND LINDA VAN DEURSEN

who killed the paper ?

Red and Blue Scales, a succession of harmonious proportions, relating to the human body.

IN WHAT WAY does the size of paper relate to a human body

There were situations where I knew the work wasn't going to push the edge enough, because I still felt comfortable with what Rick was developing conceptually. And when it was to the point where I started to feel a little bit uncomfortable, or even anxious over it, then I knew that the end result would be much richer.

I can — there were times when — I couldn't get a point across to Rick of how important it was to do something for all of the audiences, which is one of the struggles with paper promotions — you have multiple audiences. And ultimately, most of the pieces are created with the designer in mind, but not everyone thinks or understands the layers of what's necessary in order for it to be appealing to the designer.

So Rick and I would just get to — it would really — not ever be combative, but it would definitely be a struggle in order for me to conceptualize. And that's that whole thing of me trying to get inside his head so that I could see why he felt what he wanted to project was important.

And, you know, similar to what Kathy says, we have to call it "quits," and then talk another day — you kind of get to that point. Because I also think that that allows the muse to come in and…

Right.

…maybe make some changes, or provide some input that's a little bit different.

And I've also learned over the years with Rick that he tends to pick his battles. And there are many times when — and it is very true — I have to get right to the edge.

And when Esse — Esse specifically — was first introduced, it was designed by designers for designers. And it was very designer focused.

THE DISCOMFORT ZONE

So we knew three or four years ago that we had to try to get a better balance. And to Su's point, it's very difficult in this market to please all three constituencies — printers, designers, and merchants.

And what I have found is, if there's a message, or a point that Rick is very stuck on, or very strong in his beliefs, he won't back off. And I have learned then to trust. Those are the times when, if we can't come together and feel good about it, I will typically back off, because I know that if it's not a matter of design integrity, he will back off and yield to me.

And I've learned, when he absolutely insists, to just stop…and then I die. *laughs* I die. I just…I'll screen my phone calls for four days after it goes out to the sales force, because I just don't want to hear any complaints. But it comes out. In the end, it's always beautiful. It works. You just learn to back off and trust.

And the way that we both got there, Kathy and myself, was because Shirley Jean actually had to pave the way, because the initial launch book of Esse was beyond anything that anyone had ever seen. So I think it's important for Shirley Jean to…

…talk about the rest.

Well, you know, I have to admit that I never felt too much anxiety. I think what I had going for me was the fact that I saw that wastebasket moment happen. I saw the president of Gilbert and the VP of marketing jump on board.

We also had, at that time — I think it was a kind of subcommittee of two or three designers from different parts of the country who helped us in the selection of Rick for this project. And I could just see everybody else's trust. And I trusted those other people's judgment, so that I didn't have to second-guess.

Did you ever second-guess when you started seeing the artwork and it was as far-out and whacked as it was at that time, for that era?

I didn't, except…once in a while I had a phone call. It was some feedback that one of you had heard from the community about the cover artwork, in that it resembled the female anatomy. You remember?

I remember that.

And that was the only time that I ever questioned, and that was only because someone else had seen something that I totally never saw, and so it never concerned me. But no, I didn't really have any concerns about the frontier of the design because I knew what we were — I knew what we had hired. I knew what Rick was.

FRIENDS OF GILBERT_PUBLICATIONS DESIGNED BY (FROM LEFT) J. ABBOTT MILLER, CHESTER, ED FELLA _1995-96

PRESS CHECKS

Rick knows exactly what he wants on press, so he's very definitive. He gives great guidance. He totally understands the process, so again, you feel really comfortable. But I can remember sitting with the printer a few times and Rick would take a look at a press sheet, within seconds be able to note what might need to be changed, and then they would just move on, bring it back into the press room. He's not controlling, kind of in your face in the press room. He's just very respectful of whoever the press operator is and just is able to articulate what he's trying to achieve — and they get it.

I remember being on some of the — my very first press checks were with Rick, and so it was sort of a learning ground for me. And I can remember the one advice that — piece of advice that he had given me. And that was, you know what you want, but don't ever pretend to know how to get it, because you don't know how to get it. That's why those experts are here. So it's important for you to say "It needs to be warmer" or "I think it needs to be more vibrant."

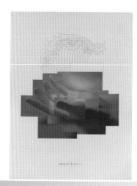

But don't tell them to turn something up, say, more red and yellow, because you're going to alienate them.

Let them know what you need, and let them be the experts to solve it, and you will get much further.

There with the trust again.   Good advice.

Yeah.

"I can assure you this IS award winning stuff."

"I don't know. It doesn't do anything for my little general—does it do anything for your little general?"

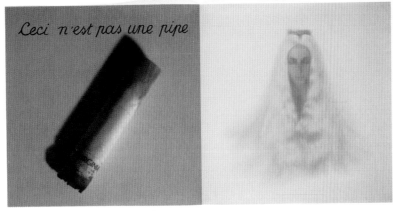

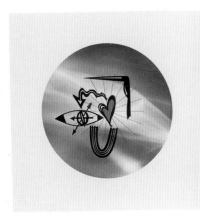

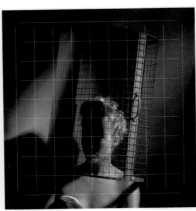

I LOVE YOU

FUTURE FASHION

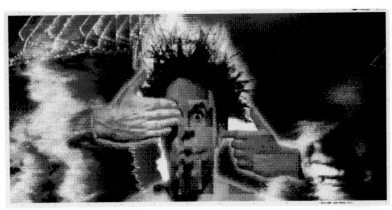

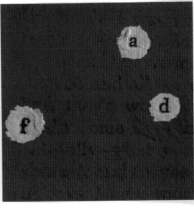

BASTA

DETAIL

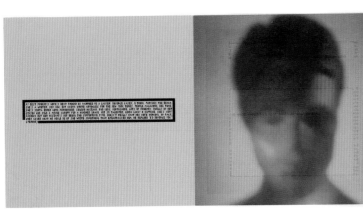

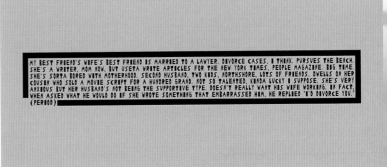

GIVE & TAKE_ESSE PROMOTION FOR AUSTRALIA/NEW ZEALAND WITH FOLDER_1992

CLOSING THE CHAPTER

The most difficult moment, and I guess it's not really difficult with Rick because we're pretty open and honest with where we are — but sometimes the most difficult part for me is a defense mode that I have to go in occasionally with our sales force or with the merchants. And that goes back to the meeting that we had three or four years ago with Rick. If they don't get to experience him or know him, they don't have the appreciation level, I guess. And so sometimes it gets — sometimes I feel like I have to protect him — protect him from the sales force and vice versa. And that can get painful sometimes.

The worst moment for me was not working with him but departing from the relationship. Really. It was very difficult. And as funny as it sounds, I can remember saying, how will I be able to go a week without talking to him?

And even beyond that?

And so, I promised myself that for the first month or so I would have to talk to him every Friday.

To get your fix for the weekend.

Yeah. Because you do become so close, like Kathy said earlier. It's a friendship level that you develop, too. So the relationship deepens, and it's really — that was the difficult part.

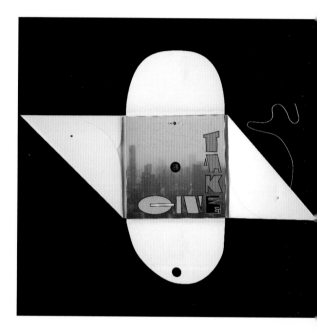

Yeah. I didn't work with Rick long enough to develop a close friendship, but I did feel like we had certainly shared some moments. I mean, we talked about our tastes in music, for example, over lunch one day. And this was supposed to be a business meeting, and it turned out to be just chatter between friends. And even when I did — when I was leaving Gilbert — I did feel like there was a sense that this, that I would miss the friendship. And I didn't quite know how to deal with that, because I wasn't — I had never really made friends with someone who I had hired before.

GILBERT

GILBERT

BE GREAT

BACKWORD

RICK VALICENTI
THIRST
1 JANUARY 1996

Capturing an audience of respectable measure by employing modern typographic styling has long been considered the avant thing to do. It is, however, my seasoned opinion that this risk-driven method of response retrieval is no longer on target.

After almost two decades of beating my head against the wall, I've come to believe the 'safe' approach yields the most certain communication subversion.

If I've been told once, I've been told a zillion and one times, "they just won't get it." In hindsight, I'm amazed at how resistant I was to this insight. The enlightened audience for whom I once designed and experimented seemed to be shrinking.

fig.1
ONCE CLOSE TO THE
LUMBERING PREY,
THE DETERMINED WHITE
TIGER SHEDS ITS
CUDDLY, CUTE, FURRY
DISGUISE AND BEGINS
TO GNAW AWAY WITH
A RAW AGGRESSIVE
KILLER INSTINCT.

Commerce had hypnotically numbed the universal sensibilities of design's potential audience, rendering the majority alert only to a vocabulary of dumb and dumber under the foil-stamped patina of process colors. No wonder the only audience I could speak to was other designers! *Talk about howlin' at the moon!* DUH!

The exact moment of awakening alludes me, but when I did come out from under my avant-glaze, I had gained a new found formula for spreading the messages of real value *and* be understood by the multitudes. I call my new methodology: THE WHITE TIGER. Allow me to share its genesis. The notion comes from a network television special featuring Siegfried and Roy, the flamboyant Las Vegas illusionists. Siegfried (the blond one) welcomed me to his world. Mysteriously lit by candles and wearing a crimson velvet smoking jacket, he delighted in a home video of Roy romping with their (once) ferocious White Tigers. Siegfried reminded me not to be fooled by the soft white fur and gentle ways, for the White Tiger remains a dangerous animal (even though the lobotomy incisions seemed apparent to me).

On any day along the moving walkway into the Las Vegas Mirage Hotel and Casino, the magic White Tigers are on display in a McDiznee™ world of fantasy faux. The hotel guests are seduced by the barely breathing specimens to purchase souvenirs stuffed in their likeness.

This nonstop parade to the cash register showed me the key: "Rather than make my valued messages look risky, edgy, and new, I now know to cover them in the familiar warm and soft look of The White Tigers."

To the point, who in their right anesthetized mind wants to snuggle up to the unfamiliar?

Behavior patterns are indeed programmable. Zappy Meals™ and the thoughts of Ratman™ Returnz have us salivating like dogs and picking at each other like chimpanzees. The fat cats and their minion gurus have had their way with damned near everyone's uncommon sense. The White Tigers' touch remains the only way to defibrillate mass culture's heart, a Trojan horse approach of sorts.

BUY THIS NOW! YOU NEED THIS NOW!

HURRY, TIME IS RUNNING OUT ON THESE INCREDIBLE SAVINGS!

WE'VE GOT WHAT YOU'RE LOOKING FOR!

Now doesn't the familiar sound really comfy? Too bad the message sucks!

Please take a minute to check your pulse.

If your glazed-over stare upon the purple mountain majesty of the promising land seems a bit out of focus and illuminated with the orange glow of strip mall signage, marketing's mind control may already have put you under its hypnotic spell.

Good taste in today's modern land o' bland culture is served presweetened and pulp free (that means without pulp). Should you think you are in control of your senses, know that Mr. Big, Inc., perceives you to be really stupid. So stupid, in fact, he thinks you're returning calls and expecting your money back. I'm sorry if I've offended you, but actually, it's much worse than that; Mr. Big, Inc., feeds off this control to the point that he's got you throwing rocks at the ground and missing.

Verily, I speak the truth. Should any among you choose to mount an offensive (or in this case, a self-defensive), remember that only the warm, fuzzy, and familiar can serve your effort to communicate any messages of real value.

Dress those treasured messages of hope and wisdom as White Tigers. If they don't look like White Tigers, no hypnotized victim of commerce will be enticed to cuddle up close enough to them for you to snap 'em out of it ... and if it's too late and the damage is done: *BITE THEIR HEADS OFF!*

Well, the *I.D.* magazine ads — I can recall a moment in advertising in *I.D.* magazine, the image was based on — gosh, I don't remember exactly what it was. It was, I think, a dog and there was blood, and Rick had found it at a flea market one weekend. Do you remember that, Kathy?

No, but this sounds very familiar.

MAGAZINE ADS

But anyway, Rick saw something in that image, and for some reason it resonated with him. It was a framed image. He bought it, and then he used it for one of our ads. And it definitely caught your attention. It didn't relate at all to paper being the product that was being promoted, and we got a lot of negative feedback on that because people thought it was too violent. And so, really, the posture we had taken with those ads was to be jarring. For the most part, they were all quite jarring, including the ones for *Wired*. I mean, *Wired* was, at that time, a new publication. People were embracing it, and no paper company advertised in it. And so it really was a canvas for Rick to be able to do what he wanted to do, using technology, because it was so appropriate for that vehicle.

Can I ask a question?

Did the people who gave you criticism on those ads, did they ever understand the rationale for choosing the ad, and for choosing the vehicle?

For *I.D.* magazine, it was just, let's make sure that we're out there. People are going to notice our ads. Let's shake things up and get ourselves in this magazine that was really much more across many, many design elements, and not just paper. We've since, of course, been followed by many other paper companies advertising. And *Wired*, I also looked at *Wired* as a vehicle for Rick to really stretch design. Most of the criticism on the ads came from people who actually received the magazine, not from anyone internal…One of the ideas we debated quite a bit was "Design is mainstream, but good design isn't mainstream." And how could we take what we had and bring it to more people in a better form so there was less mediocrity?

Oh, I see.

We really were testing as many vehicles as we could in order to get the word out there. And you know, it was during my reign there, part of what I wanted to happen was for Rick to almost be synonymous with Gilbert. So if people saw his work, they thought Gilbert. And what Gilbert has been able to do is create things that are definitely edgy and make people think, and take a little more time to present and more time to understand.

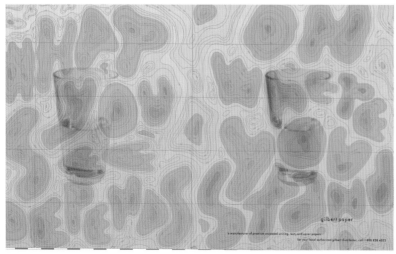

be cause

NOTHING BUT THE TRUTH

EXHIBIT A : GUILTY BY REASON OF INSANITY

Richard N Bianco

ATTORNEY AT LAW
Gary Indiana

So you're looking for THE TRUTH. Well, right after you find the Loch Ness Monster, the right health care plan and Madonna's sincerity you'll find THE TRUTH. It's not Black & White it's Smoke & Mirrors.

Did David Copperfield really make the big French lady disappear in New York Harbor or is his relationship with the beautiful German girl an illusion?

Did the King of Pop marry the King of Rock's daughter because: A) 2 mixed up kids found true love while swapping dysfunctional family stories, or B) so they could create the biggest music catalogue the world has ever seen by combining the Beatles music (which he stole from Paul), Elvis' music (which she inherited after E exploded from a lethal dose of twinkies, seconal, and rhinestones) and Jackson music (which he created before taking up permanent residence on Planet X).

The principal players in these stories of major international significance don't know the answers. So what are the rest of us supposed to believe as we sit at the other end of the media and tabloid food chain?

Why did you get married or divorced or stay single or live some crazy combination of these choices. Why do you live where you live, work where you work and bed who you bed. Come on, let's go, hurry up I need answers in 25 words or less and/or a 15 second sound bite. Everything must seem that simple because everything is too complicated. ("I know O.J. couldn't have done it. All these years I've watched him score all those touchdowns and star in those cute little commercials.")

printed in usa on gilclear® heavy
GILBERT PAPER

Did I write this to spread "the truth" or to collect an easy paycheck. Are you reading this because you want to stay on the cutting edge of the design world or because you have 5 minutes to kill till lunch.

We are complex creatures living in a complex world. The stress and confusion makes us sick and then kills us. Choose your medicine—drugs, religion, alcohol, exercise—it's not enough. We've got to simplify things.

Health care, Bosnia, gun control and abortion are way too complex. So let's spend our time relaxing with Eric & Lyle, O.J.'s trial, and Ann Nicole Smith's denial. ("I did not marry an 89 year old Texas billionaire for his money. I truly love, worship and adore his frail, wrinkled, wheel chair bound body.")

The truth is very complex and elusive. It's like white light filtered through a prism, a whole rainbow of color shines through. But, if you only look at part of the spectrum then you think it's all blue, she thinks it's all red and he thinks it's all green. To truly see the whole rainbow you have to slow down, step back and carefully study the whole complex scheme. Way too complicated for our quick fix world.

The Dean of trash celebrity, Chuck Manson, has been on the interview circuit lately to commemorate the 25th anniversary of his Slaughter of Innocent People Tour. (Book, Movie, 5 CD Box Set—who knows) Members of the press are, of course, tripping over each other to talk to this national treasure. In a recent interview Mr. Manson stated, "I was crazy when it meant something to be crazy—nowadays EVERYONE'S CRAZY." *Now that's the truth.*

NOTHING BUT THE TRUTH

EXHIBIT B : COLLEGE=SUCCESS=$=HAPPINESS

Richard N Bianco

ATTORNEY AT LAW
Gary Indiana

From our earliest memories in brand new post World War II suburbs the "born at the right time generation" was told, "Get an education, work hard and the whole world will be yours." So we went off to college in numbers too big to ignore. Some to avoid sending an R.S.V.P. to the Johnson-Nixon Rice Bowl Party. You know, the one that gave D.C. a new tourist attraction with the names of 50,000 party guests etched in black marble. Some to feel the sex, drugs and rock and roll explosion from ground zero—a 60's college campus. Some to be good little kids and get a good education just like mommy and daddy said.

So we took out our student loans, grabbed our lava lamps and notebooks and created THE SIXTIES. We got our B.A.'s, B.S.'s, Ph.D's and M.D.'s with our right hand while we thought we stopped the war and changed the world with our left hand.

On graduation day we asked what line do we get in for the $100,000 a year job. Unbelievably large numbers of the Boomer Generation got what they asked for. Good jobs, great spouses, 1.8 children and a white picket fence. The Ford station wagon of our childhood became the Dodge Mini Van which became the Jeep Cherokee.

We had it all—money, family, success, everything our GI billed fathers told us we could have—and more, much, much more.

It's all an illusion. Behind those white picket fences and inside those shuttered windows of the double mortgaged, two income eating homes lurks the most stressed out, drug addicted, divorce crazy generation in history. We're the Boomers—we do everything bigger.

Manicured front lawns in the "right" neighborhoods and membership in the "right" country club must be fed with 18 hour work days and 24 hour stress days. The truth is, behind the mahogany front door in the finest neighborhoods you're likely to find an aging, disillusioned boomer living out his life in quiet desperation. "I did all the things I was supposed to do so why am I so unhappy."

printed in usa on gilclear® heavy
GILBERT PAPER

Why did the illusion we chased turn out to be such an ugly reality. Simple. Our post World War II parents bought into an illusion (College=Success=$=Happiness) and served it to us as if it was №1 on The Mosses Stone Top Ten List.

This is not to blame our parents. Most of them did not have a college education or much money and they truly wanted their kids to have a better life. Better education and better jobs seemed like the route to be sure "my kids get what I never had".

And basically they were right. But they didn't factor in how greedy, selfish and spoiled our generation would become. Most of us grew up in a small 3 bedroom house with 1 bathroom, 1 car, 1 black and white TV (eventually replaced by the miracle of "living color") and 1 phone (black rotary dial).

Today, however, most bulging (at the waist) boomers require the following: a 4 bedroom house (with a 6 figure mortgage), a 3 car garage, 2 1/2 baths, central air, 60 inch projector color TV, an assortment of other color TV's and VCR's scattered throughout the house (minimum 1 per family member), computers (a variety of lap top, desk top, CD Rom, Sound Blaster accessories), private trainer for Dad, aerobics for Mom, soccer for Jason and ballet for Jennifer.

Now here's the ugly truth. The joke is on the boomers. In 1959 the boomer's dad drove home from an 8 hour a day job (when's the last time you only worked 8 hours) in the family car (which was owned not leased) and had the time, energy and peace of mind to truly know and enjoy "the family" before they all peacefully sat down in front of the black and white TV in the same room at the same time. We've sure come a long way baby.

Anyone know how we can get back to where we once belonged?

TRUTH_gilclear promotion_1994

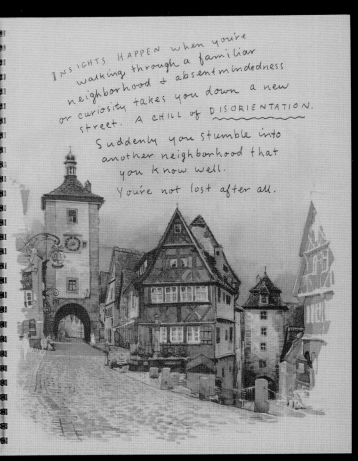

INSIGHTS HAPPEN when you're walking through a familiar neighborhood & absentmindedness or curiosity takes you down a new street. A CHILL of DISORIENTATION.

Suddenly you stumble into another neighborhood that you know well.

You're not lost after all.

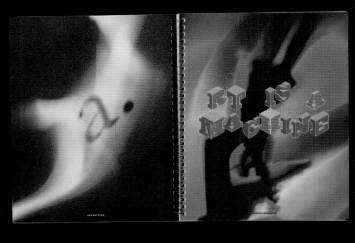

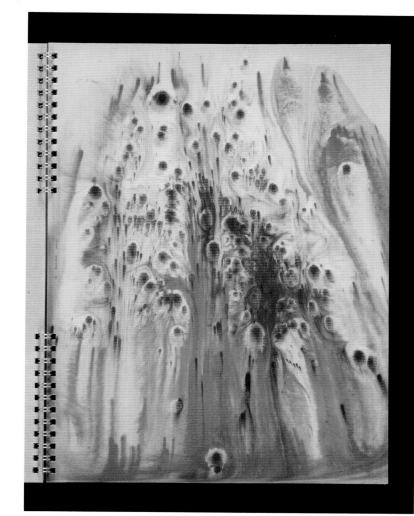

TRANSLUCENCE_ GILCLEAR AND CLEARFOLD PAPER PROMOTION_1998

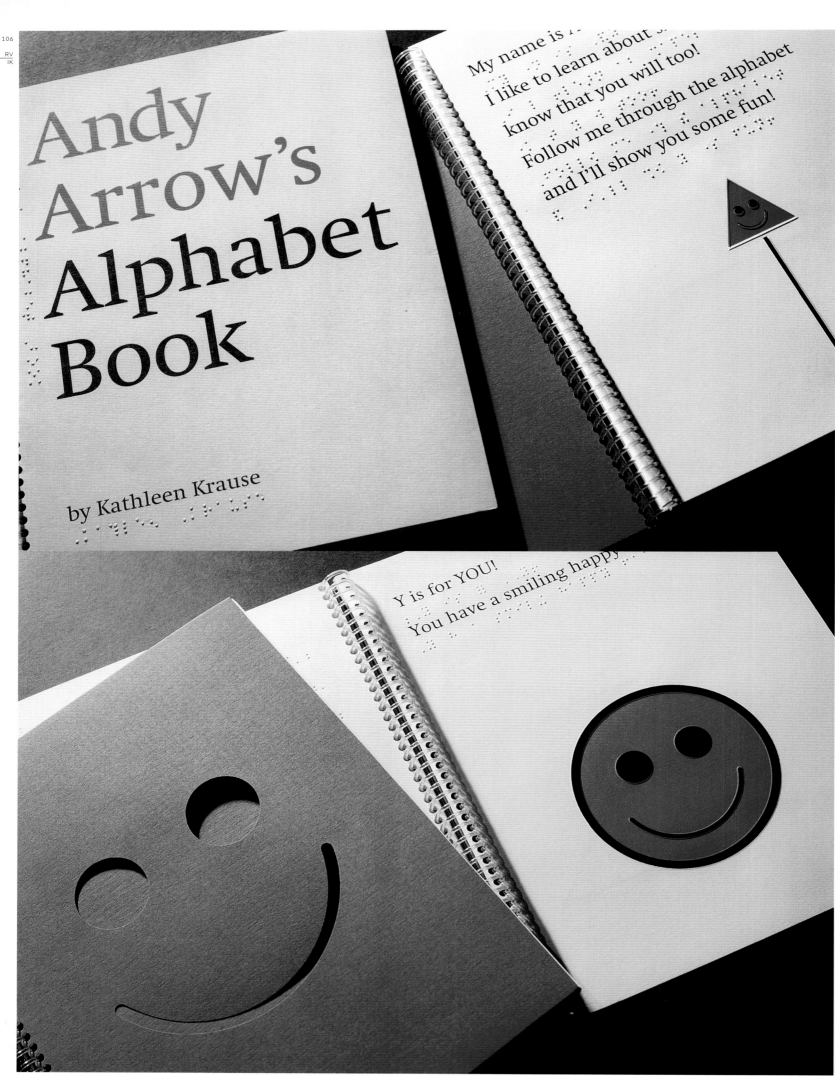

Andy Arrow's Alphabet Book

by Kathleen Krause

My name is *[text obscured]*
I like to learn about *[text obscured]*
know that you will too!
Follow me through the alphabet
and I'll show you some fun!

Y is for YOU!
You have a smiling happy *[text obscured]*

ABOVE: ANDY ARROW'S ALPHABET BOOK_FUNDED BY GILBERT'S "SMART DESIGN" CHALLENGE FOR SIGHT-IMPAIRED STUDENTS_1994; RIGHT: ESSE PRINT DEMONSTRATION_1991

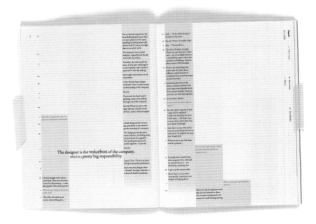

PAPER ON THE WEB

Kathy, where's your market on the web?

Is it merchants?

Is it designers?

Is it printers?

Is it all of those people?

Primarily, it's the specifications side, so it's primarily designer focused. But it's also educational based for the designers. It's pretty straightforward, but it's not just a paper mill on a web site.

Okay.

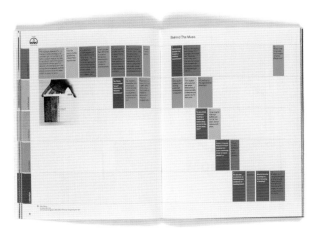

You can find very tactical information, very straight-forward production tips, the stocking of the grades, etc. And then you can go into what we call the Gilbert Diner, which is very sort of creative and kind of wacky, and so you can go wherever you're comfortable. We won awards — web awards. It's been incredibly well received. I've heard from different people in the industry that many times our web site is used sort of as the benchmark…

It is (was) a benchmark web site.

I would agree.

Yeah…

It is?

Great.

Yeah.

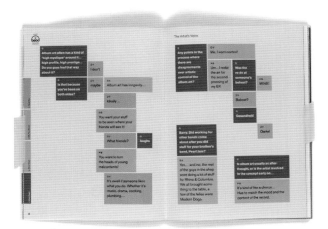

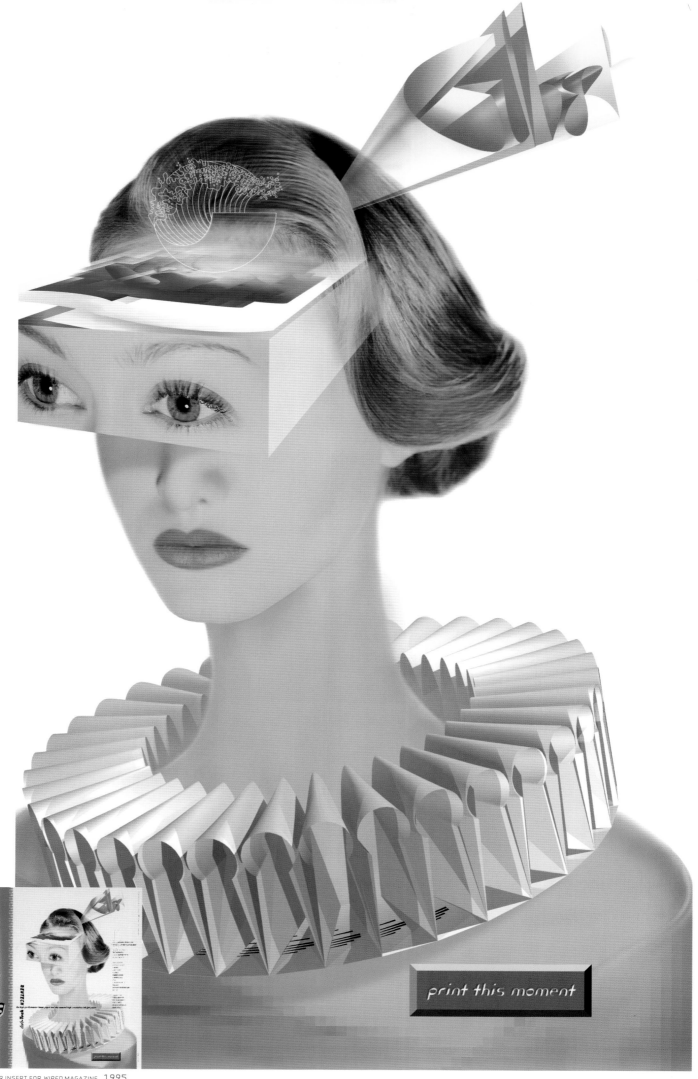

PRINT THIS MOMENT_POSTER INSERT FOR *WIRED* MAGAZINE_1995

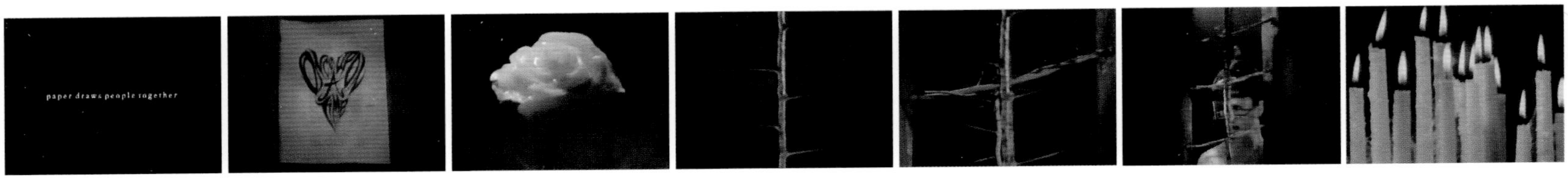

PAPER DRAWS PEOPLE TOGETHER

ONCE UPON A TIME

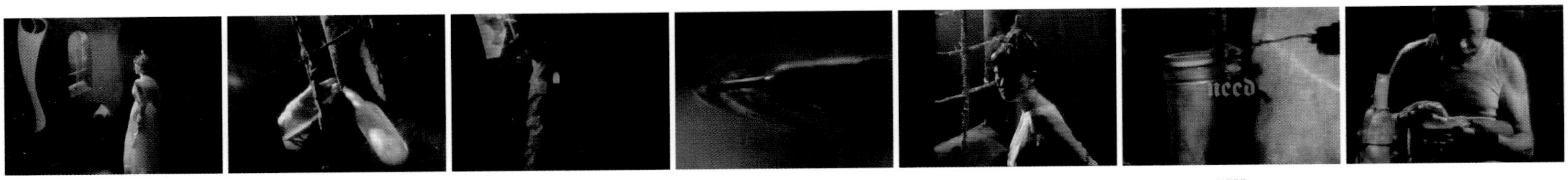

NEED

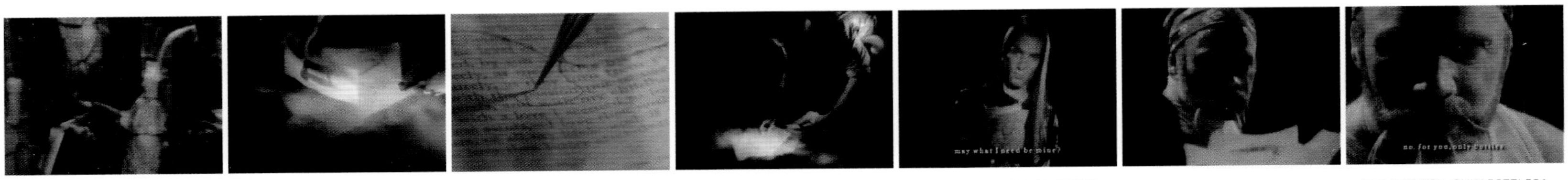

"MAY WHAT I NEED BE MINE?"

"NO. FOR YOU, ONLY BOTTLES."

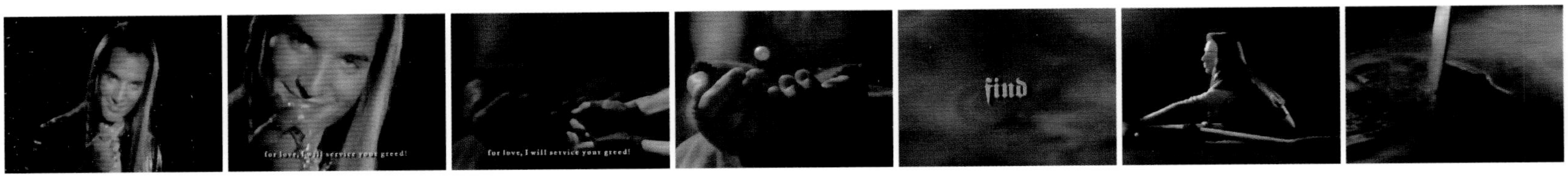

"FOR LOVE I WILL SERVICE YOUR GREED!"

FIND

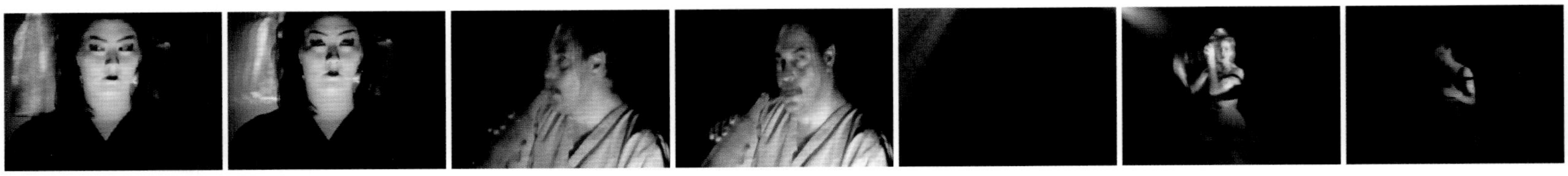

ONCE UPON A TIME _PROMOTIONAL FILM_ 1994

About the trust level — I mean, we talk about being prepared to present a project in front of people. I can't tell you how many times I've met Rick at an airport, handing off art boards on the way to a sales meeting…

Right!

laughs

…that I'm thinking, this time he's not going to make it, I'm going to die right up here, I'm going to have nothing to show. I'm going to be up here naked. And he pulls it off.

See, I think that's also an important part of working with Rick. And it's — sometimes you get brought to a point where you don't see anything until the final moment, when you really need to have a little more time with it. So in growing and strengthening you finally come to the point where, as much as you don't like it, you accept the fact that only at the eleventh hour will you receive what you're looking for. But again, you trust it so much that you know…

It'll be there.

…it's going to be there, you know?

DEADLINES AND TRUST

That would be hard for a first-time client.

laughs

I can remember the times where it's like, "Rick, I have got to deliver this piece on this day. We are down to the wire. If we don't release art tomorrow" — that kind of thing. He's going, "It's okay. We'll be fine, we'll be fine."

Yeah.

I can remember some sleepless nights, and now it's just, you go, "It'll be here."

Okay.

I guess, probably, with a lot of designers — they work better under pressure. You know, it's the whole last-minute thing. It'll be there.

PATRICIA B ROBINSON

May 18, 1952

Dear Rick,
   At last, I am officially "bronzed." This is my first letter in my new identity. Thanks for your help in making it happen!
   I continue to be thrilled for the relationship that we have with you and for the work you are doing for us. Thanks and keep it coming!

       Fond regards,
       Pat

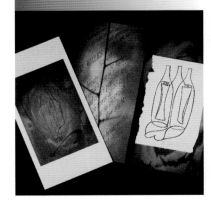

RV
C

RV
GV

RV
ES
YY
C

RV
C

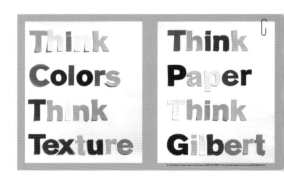

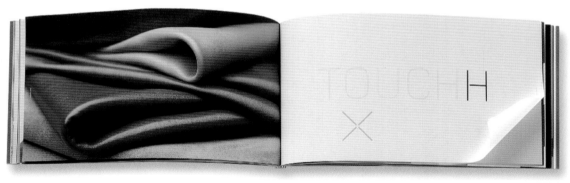

COMPROMISED?

What we found is that here we're producing these very cool pieces that are effective at the design level where they don't need a whole lot of explanation. But what we found is that the elite level of the design community is much smaller than the masses of advertising agencies and printers, etc. To be respected and loved in the design community doesn't necessarily bring the orders in at the end of the year — it's a nice thing, but you know, it's not what we're here for. And so I've done a variety of videos, the real classic home video where it's me in the conference room and an amateur video camera saying this and this and this, and all the way to scripts. I pick Rick's brain: "What were you thinking, what were you doing, and why was this and blah-blah-blah?" And then I'll put it in layman's terms, so that those who are not at the elite design level can understand. And Rick will take a peek at it, and he'll make sure that I'm accurate with what I'm saying, and then I'll go ahead and publish that. Because if the merchants aren't comfortable presenting edgy pieces they won't use them.

Kathy, do you feel that Rick ever in the design process felt that he wasn't true to his design form, in the end, with the final piece?

No.

No, okay.

No, and I guess that goes back to picking the battles. Rick will give, I take — my style is much more pragmatic and much less cutting-edge design, I think, than Shirley Jean and you, Su. And so he has sort of evolved to that, but there are times when he just shuts me down and says, "Kath, this is it." And he says, "Trust me. You've got to trust me on this one." And those are the ones where I'm like, "Oh man!"

I say, "Let me go home."

And if I sleep well, and I'm not panicked — there can be a little bit of anxiety, but not like "I'm dying" — we go with it, and it's never failed.

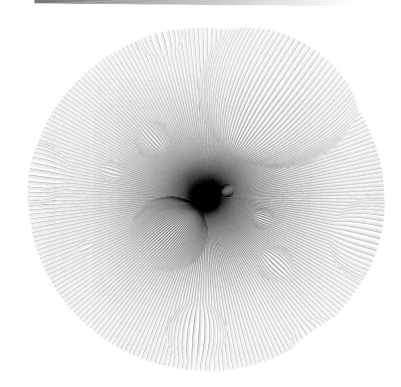

To present Rick's work to others at the company, I have to be very onboard and very comfortable. If you can stand up there in front of that group and you can show that piece and sell that piece with the passion that you have, and the conviction that you have, then it's successful. It's when you hesitate and hedge…

Right.

…that they'll eat you alive.

You learn enough about the piece that you can express it in the terms that your people need to hear.

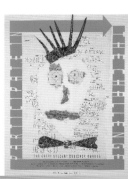

LONGEVITY

One thing, too, that I find quite amazing in this whole history of Thirst is that when we hired Rick and Thirst, we hired them solely, strictly, as a design team to help us debut Esse. And they've outlasted almost all of us here.

The company's had four presidents in that time.

The rest of us have left, and he has stayed on, and has apparently introduced several other grades for Gilbert paper. And I don't think anybody ever anticipated that he would be more than just a one-time designer on Esse. It's unusual, not only because of the design work that he does, and the purpose that he was brought in for, but I think in general, for any designer to have that kind of longevity with any company, on any project —

Yes.

Yeah, yeah.

How? How has he done that?

He's very charismatic. And he has — he has power that — it's not power in a bad way, but it's power and belief in what he does, and how he can help, that transcends whoever's there — if you can trust. That's how I see it.

I remember him as being articulate in expressing what his design is saying...

Oh, yeah.

...so that the VP of marketing did understand it. Even if he didn't get the design, he'd get the concept, because Rick could explain it.

Exactly.

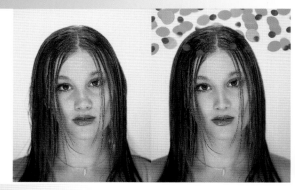

You know, there was another interesting phenomenon that took place in the course of working with Rick, and I think, Shirley Jean, if I'm not mistaken, when you started out with the whole Esse launch, you passed a lot of things through other people within the organization. As the relationship grew, it really became more empowered to the individual in marketing — totally. And I don't recall ever passing anything through for approval once you had paved the way.

And then the same still holds today. I mean, I'll take initial concepts and go to my boss and say, this is what I'm thinking, and this is the message we're going to tell, and these are the important features that I'm going to focus on.

Wow.

You can't design by committee. That's just a nasty thing. And so, it's been great that way. That's how Rick's lasted, I think. Plus he's got this innate ability to balance a friendship with business. And you really become friends with Rick. And you — and the relationship goes to another level, other than just a business relationship. And so you connect — you're in sync. And that helps. In addition to that, he can be a bit of a chameleon when he has to be. Time has changed the industry. The days of introducing a new grade and the orders just rolling, and life is great — that's so over. Now there are many different sorts of messages you have to get out there, and you have to try to communicate to the different constituents. And so, over the years, Rick has followed that path.

Fon
du Lac
Wiscon, P.
April 7th
1943
My dear Sally
well, how-r-u.
getting along
Well, I hope?.
That's good &
Expected one
letter to(x)
But none
came
at all
So I suppose
I'll have to wait
a few days. now &
and get one at the new
place I am moving To-
which is 64 W. Division St
Fon du Lac Wisconsin
U S A.
It has kept cold here
too ever since
I came except
one or two days
during the last two
days of March 1943
But I suppose Thats
how Spring comes on
just gradually easing us
Into it until the balmiest
days of June appear at
last and then we have sum
mer again. Isn't that right?
So that is the way time flies and
Seasons come and go year
by year as we journey along
P.A. E
1/But.1
than
Why so
Worried
Soon
it will
be too
hot
and
we'll
want
it cool

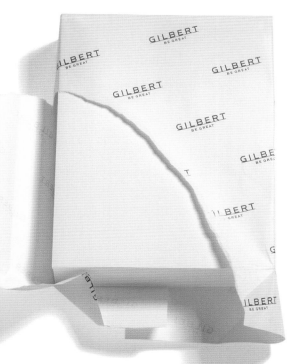

Color Clearfold

freelunch

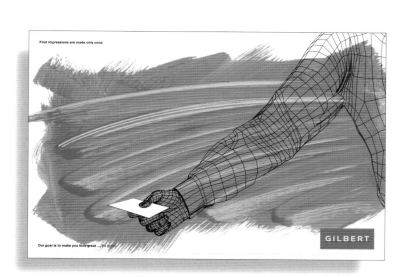

How is Thirst going to use this conversation?

WHY ARE WE HERE?

Is this going to be part of a Gilbert promotion or…

This is for the big coffee-table book about Rick and the Thirst work over the last fifteen years.

Oh, wow.

Which is 80 percent Gilbert! *laughs*

laughs

So it will kind of be a Gilbert promo, won't it?

Does that mean it'll be printed on Gilbert paper?

No one's approached me on that. I was actually…

I think it should be on coated, you would think.

Yes.

Sell that one to your managers. A whole book on Gilbert on coated. When Rick first called me and he started chatting a little bit about this, I was gearing up for the paper donation request to come. So I was — he surprised me a little bit when he took me down this avenue, that he wanted us to have this conference call.

laughs

Well, I'd love to get a copy of the book.

Oh, we all would, of course.

Yes, definitely.

It'll be our Christmas present from Thirst, guys!

Right. *laughs*

laughs

I feel like we're giving him a eulogy. Like, he died.

I FEEL LIKE WE'RE GIVING HIM A EULOGY

laughs

laughs

Did you send flowers? Because he'll be listening to this tape. Right, so let's give the dirt. What a schmuck!

PETER. ONCE THE PRESIDENT

GILBERT IDENTITY SHOWING ALL EMPLOYEES_1997

THAN

andlet'salliveinharmonywithnature'sowngranddesign.

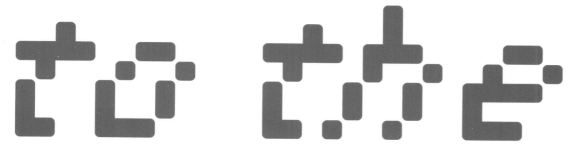

Preach-
ing

S/HE ON THE INSIDE, ME ON THE OUTSIDE
Reflections on the ideal client

For more than twenty-three years, I have served a handful of ideal clients.
In that period of time, I have experienced the other two types of clients as well:
those that "see" design's value only as a business tool; and those who "get it" as entertainment.
But rarely are there those who truly understand the intrinsic value of design…
to invisibly touch and universally connect us, one to one.
Since the mid-1970s, GOOD design has become easy to make.
However, GREAT design transcends expectations and embodies the spirit of its process.
At its best, design defines THE MOMENT, sparking meaningful discourse in its wake
and changing the consciousness of its generation.
GREAT design's presence is rare and elusive.
Today, design's client leadership is held by a precious few.
The ideal client instinctively KNOWS how to make GREAT design come to life.
The ideal client welcomes passion and encourages generosity.
The ideal client challenges designers and naysayers with intelligence and courage.
The ideal client catalyzes, isolates, and integrates the thought process.
In the end, the ideal client YIELDS to the most powerful force of all: *TRUST.*
RV_2001

to the

con-

It's always personal…

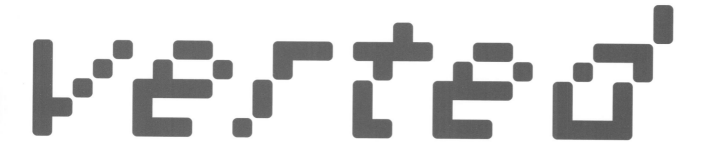

verted

Design in Heaven

I know
I know what design was like in heaven
Let me tell you about it.
Picture this.
It was white.
As far as the eye could see
there was no color…

And there's g.o.d.,
Greatest Of Designers.

g.o.d. gets the job ticket.
It says: Create the universe in seven days.
He says, "Oh shit, only seven days?"

So immediately he calls together his expert design teams…

human factors
landscape

the rest of them.

He gives them their assignments.
They all go off and do the work.
When they bring it back,
g.o.d. reviews their layouts.
Because he's benevolent,
he thinks everything's cool.

But once they had the tree,
they needed to put something on it.

g.o.d. knew from his human factors designers that they were planning oxygen-consuming species that roamed the landscape.

g.o.d. needed to feed these people with the air to breathe.

So he had to ask his environmental designers to come up with an oxygen-producing-chlorophyll-based-thing.
He didn't have a name for it then.

They came up with the leaf.
Some people on the design team came up with beautiful, symmetrical, tiny leaves.

Others came up with huge leaves.

The amazing thing was,
at least from my perspective now,
how the personalities of the various designers exemplified themselves
in the leaf designs.
It was quite exciting.

Especially when we take a look here at the beautiful symmetry of the aspen leaf, or what I think is the aspen leaf.

Its heart shape, its relationship to a New York City bumper sticker.

And the sublime relaxed contour of this oak leaf, or what looks like an oak leaf.

And the contrast of this to a maple leaf, or what might be a maple leaf.

Eventually…

The next layout g.o.d. saw was from his second-best designer.

He was from the Northeast.

He lifted the flap on his art board and displayed a white stallion.

There was this designer in the studio who kept watching both designers, seemingly without having an idea.

When g.o.d. asked him to take the flap off his art board he said,
"I've got something really, really great!"
He lifted the flap.

It was a zebra.
I love the black!
I love the white!
I love the stripes!
It looks terrific, but it doesn't go so fast.
g.o.d. thought it looked great too.

Their animal, as they had named it, was a camel.

It had two humps, long legs,

and stored "plenty of energy."

They were asked, "Why the humps?"

They replied, "For safety."

These marketing guys were asked to go back to the drawing board.

The ears had no nerve endings.

The legs were short.

The belly was big.

This animal could travel in severe heat conditions.

g.o.d. thought it was good.

They thought it was great.
Their salesmanship had surpassed even their previous efforts.
They were quite proud.

The first layout g.o.d. saw was
for the ground.
They started in the Midwest.
The landscape was pretty generic.
It looked very flat.

Can you imagine how exciting
it was when they started to talk
about mountains?

And some guy came up with the Rocky
Mountains. And another came up with
the Swiss Alps. And another said,
"Nah, nah, nah, too jagged.
How 'bout the Appalachian Mountains?"

And someone said, "Let's do glaciers.
Let's do them out of ice.
Yeah, that's what's really nice."

Then somebody said,
"How 'bout putting trees on them?
How 'bout a few trees?"

There were big trees,
little trees, medium-sized trees,
shrubs, bushes, plants…
g.o.d. loved them all.

Some were jagged.
Some were smooth.
But all of them were great.

The aggressive designer on the team
came up with man-eating leaves.

Someone came up with bug-eating
leaves. Someone came up with bugs
that looked like leaves.

Another came up with leaves that
looked like bugs.

g.o.d. thought it was all cool.

And he knew everything would
live or die based on its own aptitude
for survival.

g.o.d. asked the designer of the oak leaf
to design San Francisco.

He later asked the designer of the maple
leaf to design New York City.

The best story I heard, however…

was the one about equestrian design.

g.o.d. set the problem:
Make a four-legged
transportation system.
He put his best designers on it.

The first design g.o.d. saw was
from his best designer.
He lifted the flap on his art board
and presented the black stallion.
It was really cool!

The best part, however, was the
last presentation.

The last guys were the marketing guys.
(No design process is complete
without them.)

Their pitch to g.o.d.

(as a team)

stated that their four-legged
transportation system

had to be safe.
Their studies and surveys showed this.

Their task was to make the camel
easier to get into.

They came up with a much shorter
animal that had no humps.

They called it "another safe solution."

This animal had long ears.

It was low to the ground.
The ears were designed as handlebars
for the passenger.

These handlebars were long and floppy.

At the end, they promised g.o.d. that
they could market their animal unlike
any other product.
g.o.d. asked, "How?"

They said, "Our proposition is Another…

Safe…

Solution…A.S.S."

g.o.d. said, "Nah, nah, nah…

But thank you."

Is this you?

Faces wanted for serious photographic research

Internationally recognized designer/artist is producing a photographic documentation of **100 faces** (for no profitable purpose) which fit the following description...

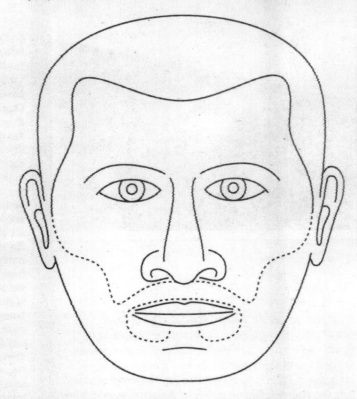

5' to 6' tall

brown or black hair

expressive eyes
(green/blue ideally)

larger than normal nose
(length and/or width)

facial hair preferred
(but optional)

10:30 am to 5:00 pm, May 31
1504 North Fremont
(2 blocks south of North Ave, 2 blocks west of Halsted, in the Weed St district, between Sheffield and Dayton)
$10 cash to the first 100 participants
Stop by, it will only take 15 minutes
Please help make this research a reality.
*When you stop by, we will take your picture, ask you to fill out a simple questionaire of likes/dislikes and sign a model release. Rest assured, your image will appear in an artistic rather than commercial context.

research by _Moving Design, founded by _Rick Valicenti / 3st.com

IS IT JUST ME? AN EXPLORATION OF (PERSONAL) IDENTITY AND THE LURE OF ADVERTISING_BOOK COVER_2003

Is it just me...

or have you ever noticed how few people each of us knows?

I often find myself in public surrounded by people I haven't met yet.

And in a crowd I always spot someone who resembles me.

In fact, the next time I notice someone sharing my physical identity...

I plan to introduce myself.

Maybe we will have nothing to talk about.

Maybe we will have everything in common.

Maybe sharing physical traits will mean other similarities.

Perhaps we'll share tastes, interests, world experiences.

his person might understand me in a very real way.

we have the same type of friends?

e we fallen in love with the same type of significant other(s)?

it be that we have something fundamental in common?

ething basic and essential?

How much do we really share?

RV

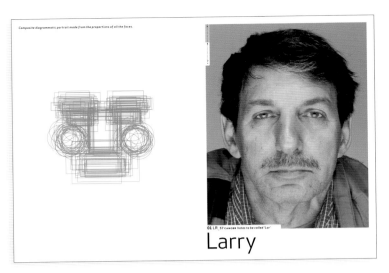

Composite diagrammatic portrait made from the proportions of all the faces.

01 LR_57 CANCER hates to be called 'Lar'

Larry

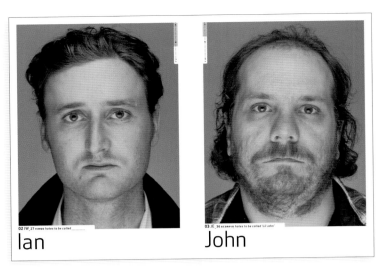

02 IW_27 VIRGO hates to be called _____

Ian

03 JE_36 SCORPIO hates to be called 'Lil John'

John

04 RG Jr._41 VIRGO hates to be called 'Glen' or 'Jr.'

Rotell

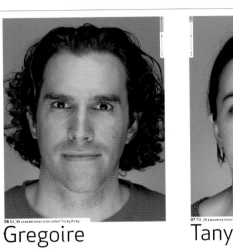

05 RI_26 CAPRICORN hates to be called 'Robbie'

Rob

06 GJ_35 CANCER hates to be called 'Tricky Dicky'

Gregoire

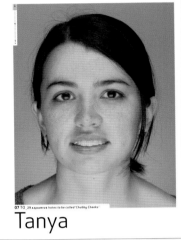

07 TO_29 AQUARIUS hates to be called 'Chubby Cheeks'

Tanya

08 TB_33 CAPRICORN hates to be called 'T-Bear'

Todd

09 SP_29 SCORPIO/SAGITTARIUS hates to be called 'Stevie'

Steve

10 ME_27 TAURUS hates to be called 'Shelly'

Michelle

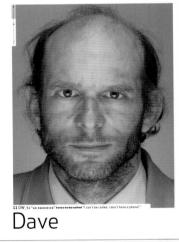

11 DW_51 "NO SMOKING" hates to be called "I can't be called, I don't have a phone!"

Dave

12 JR_52 SCORPIO hates to be called _____

José

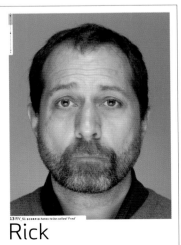

13 RV_51 SCORPIO hates to be called 'Fred'

Rick

14 DW_29 CANCER (CUSP) hates to be called "anything obnoxious"

Damian

15 MH_22 (and a few months) CAPRICORN (OR HOWEVER YOU SPELL IT) hates to be called 'P-Nut'

Matt

16 GM_34 ARIES *hates to be called "I don't know"*

Gedas

17 C_32 ARIES *hates to be called 'Eric'*

Chester

18 ME_26 NOT SURE *hates to be called 'Mike'*

Micah

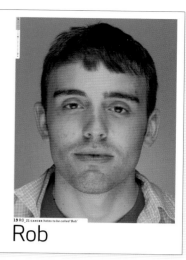

19 RO_21 CANCER *hates to be called 'Bob'*

Rob

20 JD_22 GEMINI *hates to be called Jeffrey 'Deez'*

Jeff

21 WC_25 GEMINI *hates to be called 'Billy'*

Will

22 TS_23 TAURUS *hates to be called 'Timmmmmeeeeeey'*

Tim

23 DdelR_23 PISCES *hates to be called _____*

Dave

24 KN_23 LIBRA *hates to be called "any racist slur"*

Ko

25 LG_21 VIRGO *hates to be called "I don't mind nicknames"*

Lee

26 CG_53 ARIES *hates to be called _____*

Cedric

27 TG_21 VIRGO *hates to be called 'Timmey' (South Park thing)*

Tim

28 AK_53 CAPRICORN *hates to be called ?*

Andrea

29 JR_25 LEO *hates to be called 'Jonah/'Bitch'*

Jonah

30 DS_41 CAPRICORN *hates to be called 'Homey'*

Darryl

31 OR_34 ARIES *hates to be called 'Idiot'*

Oliver

ᵒ¹ coffee, bread, cheese, cookies ᵒ² nothing–
coffee ᵒ³ bacon & egg's ᵒ⁴ scrambled eggs, toast,
bacon/sausage, milk ᵒ⁵ nothing ᵒ⁶ cashew nuts
& Raisin Bran ᵒ⁷ chai tea, cinnamon-raisin toast
ᵒ⁸ toasted whole grain bread with cream cheese
and natural peanut butter ᵒ⁹ one banana
¹⁰ ½ banana ¹¹ process cheese food (16 slices),
corn nuts, McDonald's coffee (large) ¹² chicken,
rice ¹³ Smart Cereal with golden raisins and
2% milk, orange juice, chai tea ¹⁴ Crispix w/fruit
& milk ¹⁵ nothing, just woke up ¹⁶ expresso,
brownee ¹⁷ coffee, a bit of a scone, a smoothie
¹⁸ zucini bread ¹⁹ wings ²⁰ wings ²¹ wings ²² coke, cold
pizza ²³ rice, salmon, vegetables, fruit
²⁴ 5 slices of wheat bread with apricot jam and
a cup of soy milk ²⁵ soup ²⁶ egg's, bacon, toast,
milk ²⁷ cereal, sandwitch, chips ²⁸ corn flakes
w/bananas & strawberries ²⁹ a Cliff Bar ³⁰ nothing
³¹ eggs/potatoe

question 8
What have you had to eat today so far?

ᵒ¹ chef ᵒ² rock star ᵒ³ police officer ᵒ⁴ astronaut
ᵒ⁵ _____ ᵒ⁶ inventor ᵒ⁷ teacher or cashier
ᵒ⁸ movie special effects ᵒ⁹ geometry teacher
¹⁰ oceanographer (study sharks) ¹¹ archiologist, but
I gave it up because I can't spell it properly
¹² art ¹³ never thought about it ¹⁴ law?? ¹⁵ live
¹⁶ _____ ¹⁷ architect ¹⁸ architect ¹⁹ tow truck driver
²⁰ astronaut ²¹ astronaut ²² artist/scientist/
astronaut ²³ cartoonist ²⁴ doctor/dentist or international spy ²⁵ Ringo Star ²⁶ lawyer/pro sports
²⁷ musician ²⁸ adventurer/writer/artist ²⁹ comedian
³⁰ play baseball ³¹ _____

question 15
What did you think you wanted to do for a living when you were little?

ᵒ¹ Gore ᵒ² Gore ᵒ³ Bush ᵒ⁴ didn't vote ᵒ⁵ n/a ᵒ⁶ Gore
ᵒ⁷ Gore ᵒ⁸ Gore ᵒ⁹ _____ ¹⁰ Gore ¹¹ "objection
your honour, question assumes facts not in
evidence!" ¹² No ¹³ Gore ¹⁴ n/a ¹⁵ Yes ¹⁶ _____
¹⁷ can't vote in this country ¹⁸ didn't–sorry ¹⁹ Gore
²⁰ vote? ²¹ none ²² Gore ²³ Nader ²⁴ I'm not allowed
to vote because I only have a green card
but if I could have I would have voted for Nader
²⁵ did not vote ²⁶ No Bush ²⁷ Gore ²⁸ Gore ²⁹ Gore
³⁰ Gore ³¹ _____

question 19
Who did you vote for in the last presidential election?

ᵒ¹ Judy ᵒ² Allison ᵒ³ Sharon ᵒ⁴ Emma Bushrod
ᵒ⁵ Charlotte ᵒ⁶ Robin ᵒ⁷ Doug ᵒ⁸ Sarah ᵒ⁹ Stephanie
Slack ¹⁰ Patrick ¹¹ it's rude to ask names!
(well, from ̲Her sort, anyway!) ¹² Rosa ¹³ Susie
¹⁴ K̶y̶l̶i̶e̶ Bridget ¹⁵ Ashes ¹⁶ Gabioa ¹⁷ Adrienne
¹⁸ Brooke Sorenson ¹⁹ Rebecca Morris ²⁰ Amy
²¹ Aimee ²² Sara ²³ Vicki ²⁴ ha ha, I forgot her name!
Sorry! but it was a girl I met on a school trip
when I was 16! ²⁵ Brandy ²⁶ Vanessa ²⁷ Paul
²⁸ _____ ²⁹ Sarah ³⁰ Denise ³¹ Melanie

question 21
What is the name of the first person you ever kissed romantically?

what is your name? (please print) David Whitman

what do you like to be called? Dave

what do you hate to be called? I cant be Called, I Don't Have a Phone!

how tall are you? (please circle your approximate height below)
- 4 ········ (5) ········ 6 ········· 7 ········· 8 ········· 9+

where were you born? N.Y. N.Y.

how old are you? 51

what is your sign? "No smokeing"

what have you had to eat today? Process cheese food (16 Slices)
Corn nuts, McDonalds coffee (Large)

have you traveled outside of the U.S.? Yes (why do you Ask?)
if so, where have you gone? South Pacific, (Tahiti, Fiji, Australia, New Zealand, New Caledonia, VANUATU) France, Germany, Italy, Switzerland, Sweden, Denmark, and Ide only Go to Mexico to Buy Medicine otherwise ~ forget it!

do you have a pet? (please circle all that apply)
cat   dog   (other)   no, i'm allergic
if yes, what is its name? Its An imaginary Friend. Sometimes its A Doggie, Sometimes its a "Pussey"

are you a...? (please circle all that apply)
parent   sibling   spouse   (other) "Non-Entity"

are you? (please circle one)   employed   (unemployed)
if employed, what kind of work do you do? Self Employed, I'm - an Artist, Wich is Just As good as being Un-Employed

does this look like you?
please circle the appropriate number below.
(you may modify the face, if necessary.)

Dermatitus   Fuzey EyeBrows indicating a total "fuck-up"   "a few Stragglers"   Furrows, Fill with PHiladelphia cream cheese.   EAP HAIP

1 (nope)
2   LoNg Greasy
3   UNKempt
4
5
6   Rosencia!
7
8   Long, Riddled
9   With CRATERS
10 (hey man, that's me)   Like the Moon
Like A FucKing "Gargoyle"   curved, They want let Me Join the KKK!

how much schooling have you completed? (please circle all that apply)
(3 years)
(high school)   jr. college   college   master's   Ph.D.
other   *was it worth it? yes / no / still paying

what did you (or do you hope to) study in school?
General Studys. I Dont Remember Much About it.

what did you think you wanted to do for a living when you were little?
Archiologist, but I Gave it up, because I Cant spell it properly.

what are you good at? Comedy. Theatrre! Drawing, Cooking, Film critique.

what makes you happy? Knowing That (Soon, it will be "all over") (HAHAHA!) ← MANIACAL LAUgH
(I Decline To Elaborate!)
(HeeE HeeE HAHA ← Same Laugh, but with Hands on Hips, And Echo chamber Sound Effect

who did you vote for in the last presidential election?
Objection Your Honour. Question Assumes Facts Not in Evidence!

what 'type' of person are you? (please circle one from each pair)
boxers/briefs   night/morning   gay/straight   cat/dog
wine/beer   smoker/non-smoker   other?
Smelly UN-Kempt Fuck up, Tedious, Scarry Weird! Just So Worm Like! Part RAT other part RAT!
what is the name of the first person you ever kissed romantically?
Its Rude To ask Names! → (Well, from Her Sort, Anyway!)

why did you decide to stop by today?
I Really could use the Ten Dollars, and - I Love To Have an Audience! Darling I could Just EAT Applause!

do you buy the same things every time you go to the grocery store?
(please explain...) No.
My funds Are so limited, And My Existence is but a crude bit of Preformance Art

what should we have asked but didn't?
1) Could You Use more than $10? (you look like a Bum!)
2) What are The winning Lottery Numbers For today?
3) Why Dont You get a Make over? Nose Job? etc?
4) What Do You Think of When You Jerk off?

what are the answers?
1. What do You Think?
2. Ask me To morrow!
3. How Rude. Give me the Ten Dollars, And - I'm Leaveing At ONCE!
4. I'm Too Tired And unmotivated but Ide Most Likely Think of Lamb chops

All of us on the right...

All of us on the left...

All of us.

Messages of Value   Messages about Value   Messages of No Value   *Messaging really protects our way of life.*

Mea Culpa

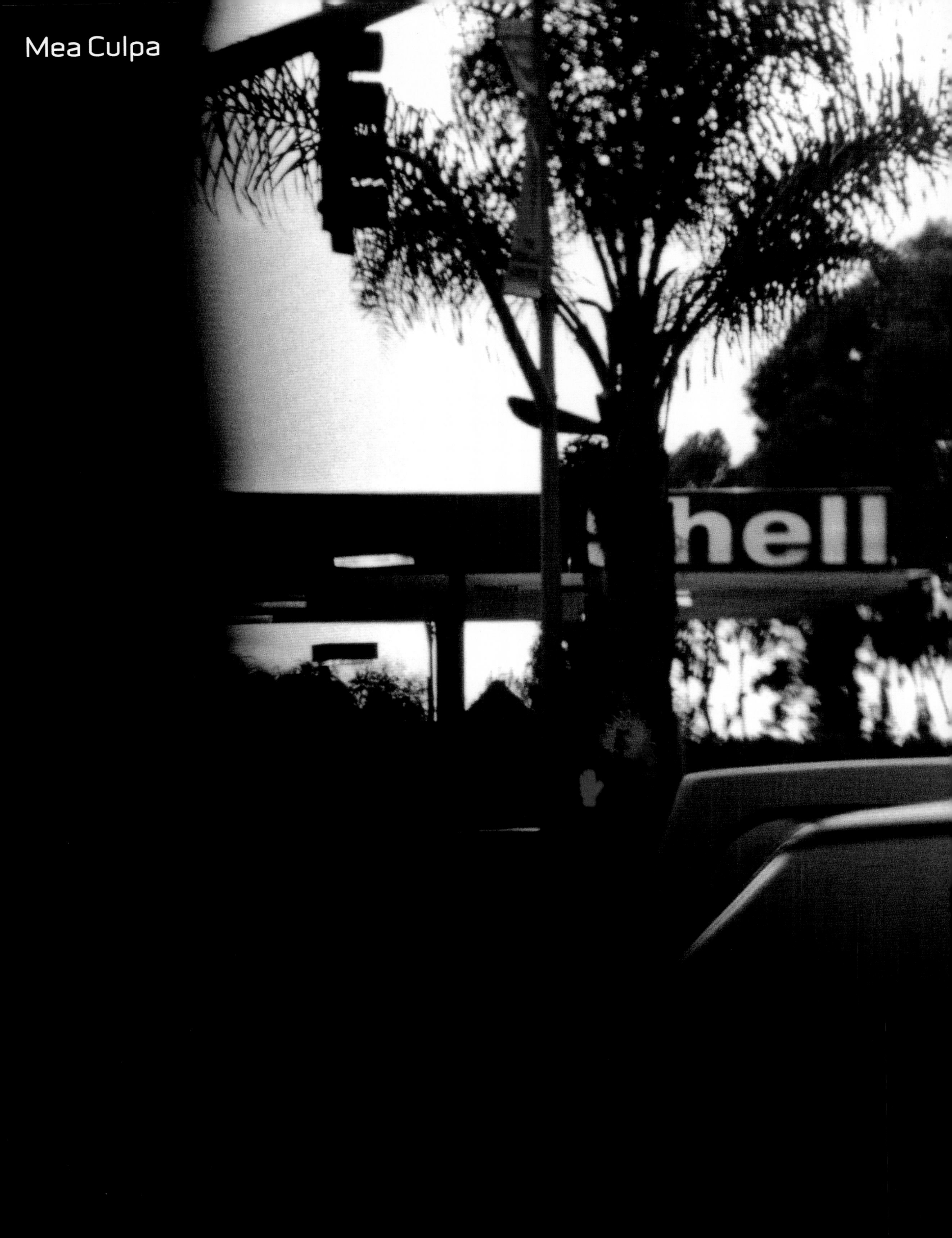

Dear World,
It's really not our fault…mostly.
Well, we probably share some of the blame
since our invoices label us as accomplices.
Sigh.

Actually, looking at the situation in the bright light
of an autumn morning in Anytown USA,
WE DESIGNERS FEEL GUILTY.

Yes, we're SORRY…VERY SORRY
for contaminating the eye and mind with all of that
"corporate messaging on steroids."

At any given moment, we were only doing our job,
TRYing TO PLEASE our clients, and maybe,
just maybe, making something we could be PROUD of.
Maybe even making something that could serve
as evidence of exhilarating creative time well spent.

The little video ad above the gas pump meter
was NOT our idea. Neither was the notion of the
ubiquitous web banner ad. But…DIRECT MAIL
catalogs and SHAMELESS consumer PACKAGING…
OUCH! Remorse.

In our defense…
POINT OF PURCHASE annoyances DO feel
like POSTER design, so that's okay. Maybe?
And that over-scaled BILLBOARD every hundred
yards on every artery into every city in every nation
on the planet is really our modern plaza KIOSK.
You know? Tradition?

The hallowed ANNUAL REPORT and hollow
capability BROCHURE are the chance for today's
opportunistic communications designer to distill
the avant-garde under the STRESSFUL PRESSURE
OF DEADLINE, CEOpinions, and shareholder zeitgeist.
Given the generous allocation of resources,
we have no EXCUSES, and we sleep well@night.

Oh, and there is modern corporate identity…
The Swoosh-envy fascination is not really our fault,
we only want our CLIENTS to be outfitted as WINners
in the high-stakes ARENA OF BUSINESS. If only
you could see how wistfully they crave to see their
names in the *Wall Street Journal*!

But, hey — T-shirts at amusement parks modeled
shamelessly by corpulent couch potatoes are
clearly the fault of sick-minded silkscreen printers
with WAY too much downtime.
The same applies for bumper stickers.

But since our profession does bestow awards
upon the disposable and ephemeral, we deserve
our CONVICTION for turning a BLIND EYE to
everything design spawns.

Sorry.

May contain nut traces. *Store in a coo*

dren. IN CASE OF OVERDOSE,

AY. Avoid contact with skin or eyes.

broken or missing. Not for aquarium

sen, ask your doctor. AVOID EX

e information. Under 2 years: Ask your de

aged. This product contains a che

fornia to cause cancer. Read instructio

ting or removing parts. CUT ALONG DOTTED LINE.

O PULL DO NOT TASTE, SWALLOW

HOLD USE ONLY. In case of accidental ingestion

tely. *Sealed for your protection.* **May be h**

ar open flame. SERVING SUGGE

against fire, electric shock and personal injury do not

quid. *Do not use appliance for other than*

18 chips. *Product settles during shipm*

not touch hot surfaces. For best before:

l dry place. Keep out of reach of chil

RADIO BY MAGNUS RAKENG_1998

GET MEDICAL HELP RIGHT AW

Do not use if seal under bottle cap is

use. If symptoms persist or wor

GENERAL BY KEVIN DRESSER_2003

CESSIVE HEAT

TWIGGIES BY RICK VALICENTI & DAKOTA BROWN_2002

See carton for complet

ntist or physician.

RHEOSTAT BY CHESTER_1997

Do not use if open or dam

SUPER DUPER BY MAGNUS RAKENG_2000

mical known to the State of Cali

ns before using. CAUTION Unplug before inser

DEE BY TRACY JENKINS_2002

Not tested on animals. LIFT TAB AN

FAUX CRA BY BARRY DECK_2002

HANDSOME BY RICK VALICENTI & BRIAN McMULLEN_1999

OR BREATHE. This PRODUCT is designed FOR house

WIT BY PAUL SYCH_1997

contact a Poison Control Center immedia

APEX SANS BY CHESTER & RICK VALICENTI_2003

armful if swallowed. Do not use ne

OZ BY PATRICK GIASSON_1999

STION for external use only. To protect

FAST GIRLS BY PATRICKING_1996

immerse cord, plugs, or appliance in water or other li

intended use. Serving size: approximately

PILOT BY MAGNUS RAKENG_1995

PUNCH BY RICK VALICENTI & GREGG BROKAW_1999

ent. OPEN AWAY FROM YOURSELF. Do

ECLOGUES BY CHESTER_1998

See side panel. Contents under pressure.

INFINITY BY CHESTER & RICK VALICENTI_2001

ART

BUSYNESS AS USUAL

FORM
FOLLOWS
DYSFUNCTION

If I do what I am told I will get a big reward.
If I do what I am told I will get a big reward.
If I do what I am told I will get a big reward.
If I do what I am told I will get a big reward.
If I do what I am told I will get a big reward.
If I do what I am told I will get a big reward.
If I do what I am told I will get a big reward.
If I do what I am told I will get a big reward.
If I do what I am told I will get a big reward.
If I do what I am told I will get a big reward.
If I do what I am told I will get a big reward.
If I do what I am told I will get a big reward.
If I do what I am told I will get a big reward.
If I do what I am told I will get a big reward.

unBranded

Gary Fisher
Age 60
Hometown Chicago, Illinois
Occupation Investment banker
Passion A thirst for speed in the great outdoors
How long have you been aware of Gary Fisher?
All of my life.
Is there anything that you'd like to say
to the younger Gary Fisher?
I'd like to thank him for naming his bikes after me.

Branded

Gary Fisher
Age 49
Hometown Marin County, California
Occupation The "first name" in mountain biking℠
Passion A thirst for speed in the great outdoors
How long have you been aware of Gary Fisher?
All of my life.
Is there anything that you'd like to say
to the older Gary Fisher?
You can be the "second name," if you'd like.

I enjoy dressing up for Halloween, or for my Thirsty friends, when they ask. But people at bike dealerships only want to see me dressed like this — in my branded riding clothes. Some dealers even went so far as to remove the pages with me in the role of Queen Isabella from their catalogs prior to handing them out to customers. Go figure.

fisher 2000.1

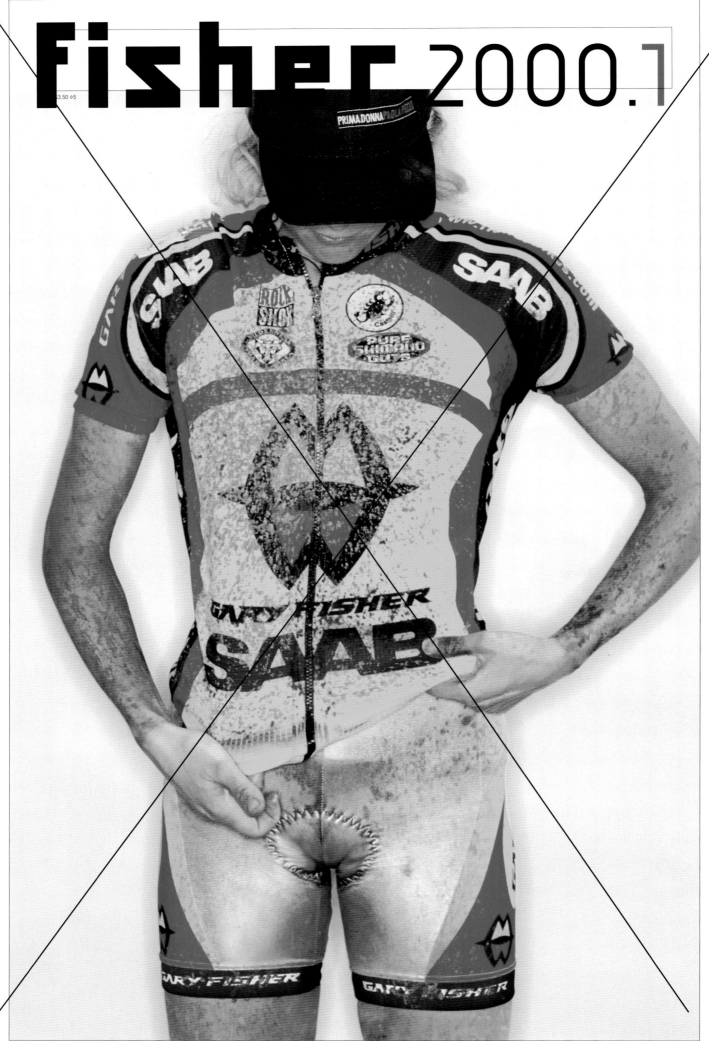

RIDERHESJEDAL

JESSSWIGGERS

JASONMOESCHLER

PATBOWER

The world of professional bike racing can be harsh, especially if you have been successful as a junior and have just graduated to the pro ranks. The circuit is kno-wn for burning up and burning out the most promising young racers. **Which is why we created the Gary Fisher/Saab U23 Racing Team — AKA "Fisher U" — a** professional team composed of the best 18 to 23-year-old riders North America has to offer. The intent is to keep racing fun, so that these promising athletes **have the chance to further their skills and realize their potential. With long-time Fisher pro and Tour de France veteran Andy Bishop serving as coach and** mentor, the team members are learning from the best. **Gary Fisher and Fisher U: The Father and the Future.** Any resemblance to actual people of any color is purely incidental. Only non-toxic paints used. Trained professionals: don't try this at home, especially if you have a white couch. Not an accurate representation of the Gary Fisher logo; do not use as a template for tattooing. (See page 16.)

Good clean product photography is important to just about all clients. We believe it's important to give the client what they like and then some.

UTOPIA

http://www.fisherbikes.com/98utopia/

LAT. 41° 58′ 08″	TEMP. 59°F/15°C
LON. 87° 50′ 47″	HUM. 43%

DATE 05/21/97	
TIME 16 : 43 : 17	

XS, SM, MD, LG, XL — SIZES
Onyx Black — COLOR
TIG-welded 7005 aluminum alloy — FRAME
Cromoly — FORK
Shimano Nexave[1] 7-speed — DRIVETRAIN
Shimano Nexave[1] V-brakes and V-levers — BRAKES
Alloy sealed front; Shimano STX rear — HUBSET
Bontrager Maverick: 32-hole front; ASYM 32-hole rear — RIMS
Tioga City Slicker; 26 x 1.5 — TIRES

[1] The Sport Utility Bike component group from
Shimano, designed specifically for SUBs.
[1] Arc handlebar is swoopy, and makes you feel like
you're going fast even when you aren't.

Good design is 90 percent perspiration and 10 percent plagiarism.
Or something like that.

NIRVANA

http://www.fisherbikes.com/98nirvana/

SIZES	XS, SM, MD, LG, XL
COLOR	Bright Green
FRAME	TIG-welded double-butted cromoly mains; cromoly rear triangle
FORK	Cromoly
DRIVETRAIN	Gripshift SRT 4.0 7-speed shifters; Shimano Alivio GS rear derailleur
BRAKES	Direct pull; direct pull levers
HUBSET	Alloy sealed front; Shimano Acera rear
RIMS	Weinmann 519: 32-hole
TIRES	Tioga City Slicker; 26 x 1.5

LAT. 41° 56' 26"
LON. 87° 43' 38"
TEMP. 57°F/14°C
HUM. 41%
DATE 05/21/97
TIME 13 : 14 : 16

¹ Taller gearing allows for higher speeds on the road.
¹ Polygon suspension seatpost takes the edge off of bumps, thereby improving the rider's life.

ZEBRANO

http://www.fisherbikes.com/98zebrano/

XS, SM, MD, LG, XL, MD-L	SIZES
Sapphire Blue	COLOR
TIG-welded cromoly mains	FRAME
Cromoly	FORK
Gripshift MRX 170 7-speed shifters; Shimano Acera rear derailleur	DRIVETRAIN
Shimano Altus CT92	BRAKES
Alloy sealed front; Shimano RH40 rear	HUBSET
Weinmann 519[1]: 32-hole	RIMS
Tioga City Slicker; 26[1] x 1.5	TIRES

[1] 26" wheels are stronger and lighter than 700c wheels, and many more tire choices are available.
[‡] Double-bend handlebar with 25° rise stem puts the rider in a comfortable, upright position.

'WISH YOU WERE HERE' *Storm Thorgerson,*
Pink Floyd Fine Art Print, limited edition of 295,
proofed, numbered and signed by the artist.

Remember always to remain totally present throughout the design process...

SEAN LENNON
INTO THE SUN

right leg
EXPERIMENT SIDE

left leg
PLACEBO SIDE

product PUMPÜUP PANTS
benefit **powerful thighs overnight**
release date **2001** (projected)
side effects **rubbery face muscles, hair loss**
International patents pending.

Styling: Mr. Ricky | THIRST | Stupid face: model's own

the competitive spirit drives research and development at the **SATISFUNCTION** INSTITUTE SECTOR G... millennial madness abounds!

n:
TESTED NEWTRITION

satisfunky

f:
FOR

u:
YOU

for immediate release: Even before founding the highly secretive SATISFUNCTION INSTITUTE*, Gary was crucial in the development of many significant advances in mountain biking. SUCH AS: the First Mountain Bike; the First Production Mountain Bike with Front Suspension; the First Production Full-Suspension Mountain Bike; Genesis Geometry; and a veritable plethora of other ATB advancements.

Recent work being done by Gary and his team of researchers (who sit at Funkification Tables) is devoted to improving the quality of bike satisFUNction through modern technology. Currently being tested are the PUMPÜUP PANTS, developed to double the strength of anyone's leg muscles overnight. Sleep in them and Get Fit For Nothin'™. Also in development: the SELF-CLEANING BIKE. They can do it for ovens, so why not bikes? A SELF-LUBRICATING component is also in the early stages of trial. At the Fisher SATISFUNCTION INSTITUTE, we care about you and the bike you ride. Ideas for a better future are welcome. www.fisherbikes.com/satisfunction/

NEVER
DO THIS AGAIN!

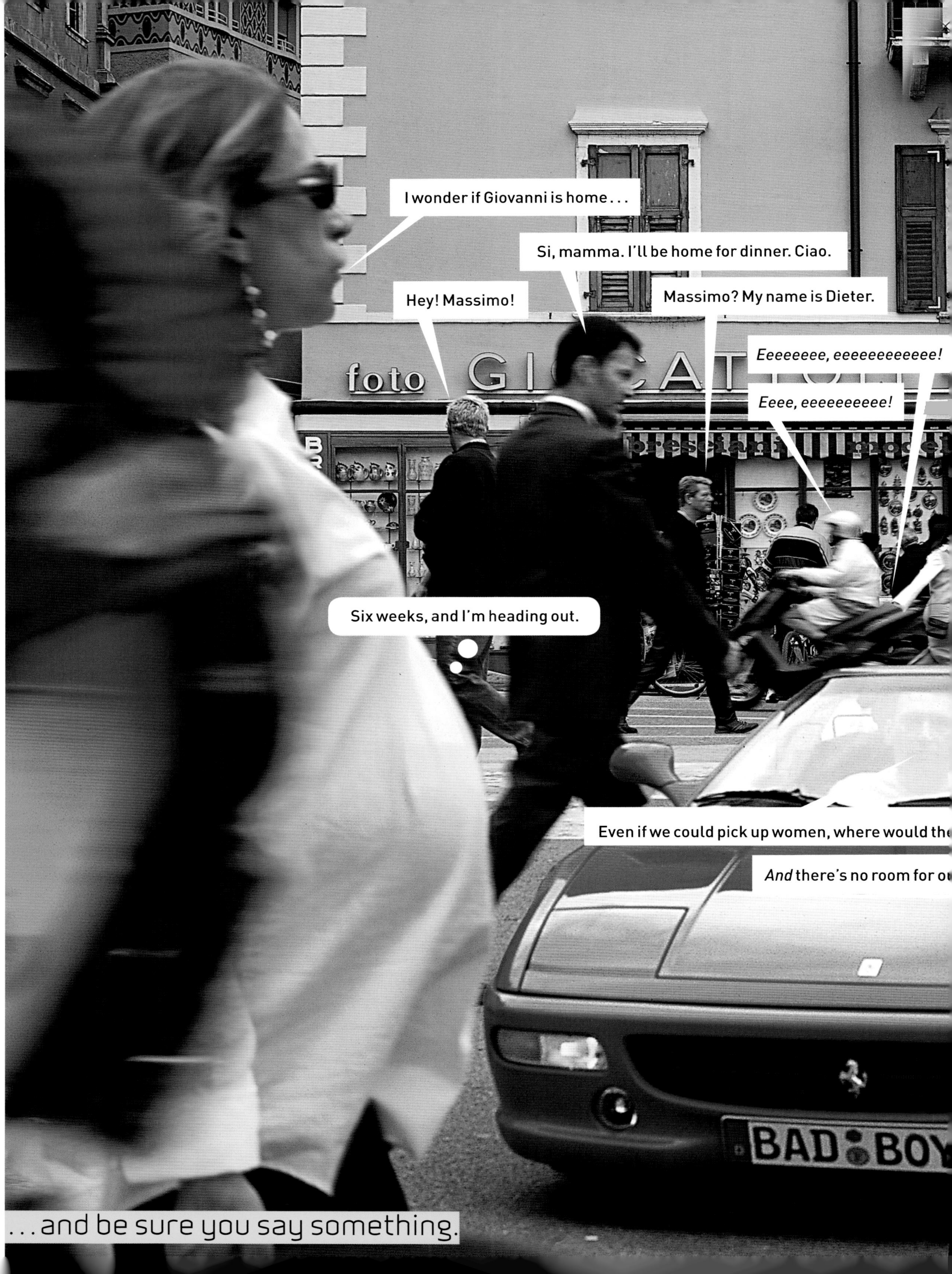

. . . and be sure you say something.

SOMETIMES LOVE FORCES PEOPLE TO BECOME GRAPHIC DESIGNERS

FOUND

The poster is what got Buster back to us. **Really?** Yep. He's an epileptic dog, so we had to get him back within 24 hours to get him his medication. So it was a very panicked situation. Plus it was super cold out. He couldn't make it through a winter night. Plus he has hip dysplasia, so he's a REAL healthy dog. **My god. How did you originally get this dog?** Actually, I met a homeless person who had a pregnant dog. I took the pregnant dog because he couldn't take care of her. **Man!** Buster was one of the puppies. Anyway, the police were zero help to the girl who found him, even though we'd called all the stations. This girl then kept him a night and saw the poster the next morning. He was gone about 23 hours...

(from our conversation with Eden, Buster's "mom")

FOUND

UNKNOWN

NOT FOUND

UNKNOWN

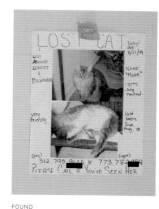

FOUND

FOUND

ENCONTRADO

RETURNED

FOUND

FOUND

FOUND

UNKNOWN

FOUND

UNKNOWN

OUND

UNKNOWN

FOUND

NOT FOUND

NOT FOUND

OUND

RETURNED

KEPT

PLACED IN NEW HOME

FOUND

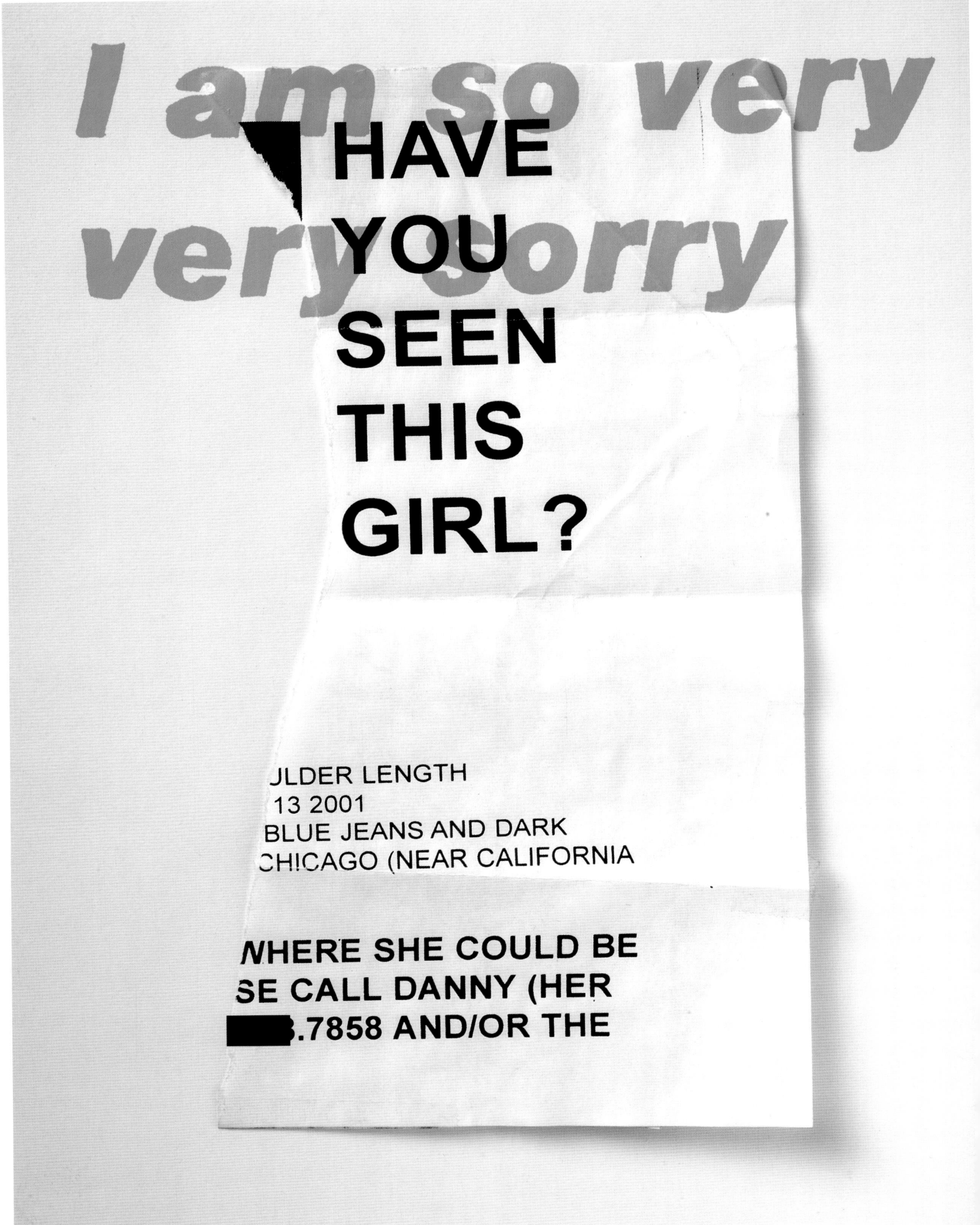

I am so very very sorry

HAVE YOU SEEN THIS GIRL?

...ULDER LENGTH
13 2001
BLUE JEANS AND DARK
CHICAGO (NEAR CALIFORNIA

WHERE SHE COULD BE
...SE CALL DANNY (HER
.7858 AND/OR THE

Nothing can take away tho... ...od ti...s... ti...it...self

MISSING PERSON

Any Information Call: (24 Hours) 805 - 685 - 7379

Any Information Call: (24 Hours) 805 - 685 - 7379

David R. W███████, age 26, was last seen Monday, July 5 at 9 PM. He drove to Lompoc, arrived safely, but no one has seen or heard from him since then. David was driving a 1993 2-door, red, Honda Civic with license plate # 3FHA644. David is approximately 6-feet tall, slim built, with medium blond hair. If you have seen him, or have any information regarding his whereabouts, please call (805) 68█████ Thank you.

Evenings alone on the couch are the worst

REWARD
MISSINGNG·DOG

- 20 pounds
- Female
- Brown w/ tan around eyes
- Hoskie Mix

- Call MINDY - ▮-868-1924
- Call Reynel - 7▮-384-8945
- Call Confusion-▮-772-7295

Or go to feast Restaurant

She's gone for good and that's bad

Lost Dog
Reward Offered

40 lb. Black Lab Mix
Silver chain no tags

Name: Java

Call (773) ▮-8789

I was more complete with him at one by my side

LOST PUG DOG

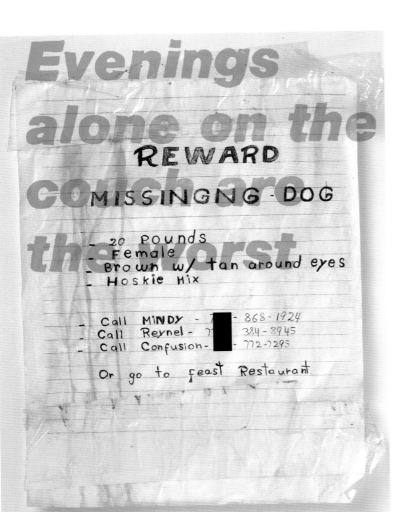

$$ REWARD $$ $$ REWARD $$

Answers to the name "Pug" or "Rex"
Last seen at St. Mary's church parking lot on Sunday
June 17th at 6:30pm. He was wearing studded dog
collar with tags. He was also wearing a leash. Tag has
old owners name and number. If found please call:
H: ▮-472-3524, W: ▮-229-8527, M: ▮-206-6177.

I just turned my back on him for one minute

$$$$ REWARD $$$$

!LOST DOG!
Small White Mixed Terrier
Answers To The Name Gringo
Lost 01-03-01
If Found, Please Call:
▮-259-5019

It was only a very small argument

$500 Reward
(We Miss Our Dog Jenna)

Looking for lost small white dog
resembeling a Poodle - Jenna is 10 yrs. old
and is in need of urgent medical attention!
Please Call
(■■) 719-6690 or (■■) 929-0142

I wish I had never ever yelled at him

$500 Recompensa
(Nosotros Extranamos Nuestro Perro)

Busco un Perro Perdido su nombre es Jenna
Es Pequeno, blanco
Se parece a una Bola De Algodon
ATENCION: Ella es 10 anos
De edad y necesita atencion medica URGENTE!
POR FAVOR LLAMAR:
(■■) 719-6690 or (■■) 929-0142

Where on earth could he be happy, but here!

Orange "Tabby" Cat
on Winchester n
Waubansi
If this is your lost
please call ■-286-1700.

Who could possibly offer more affection than me

FOUND!

A very cute,
very Affectionate,
mALe GRAy
and white
Kitty. Obviously
not a stray.
He misses his home...
Please
CAll
773-■■■-3815

I just don't understand how his ha...

WHERE IS SPECK??

He ran away.

If you see him, please call:
773 486-0420 or 773 457-9920
ask for Dave, Dustin, or Paul

Within a few moments my loved one was gone

LOST DOG

"Rocky" 6/1
Cocker Spaniel
Come home: 961-838?

Time feels so ... since he disappeared

Reward

White, Persian

LOST CAT

7█-531-6688

with lion hair cut

Life is not th... it's much harder

2 LOST DOGS
Missing since Tuesday, October 3rd

MUGSY	SPARKY
AGE 6	AGE 6
MEDIUM SIZED TIBETIAN TERRIER	TIBETIAN TERRIER MIX
TAN/ORANGE	TAN
35 POUNDS	32 POUNDS/MEDIUM SIZE

IF FOUND, PLEASE CALL
(█) 382-5812 OR
(█)382-1287

He's out somewhere ... of ... ... rest of ... cruel world

REWARD

LOST DOG

"SIERRA" 1 Y 2 YR OLD
SIBEREAN HUSKY. 40lb
FEMALE. GREY/WHT/TAN
773-█-9407

We had a cozy ... be... is an... rest of ...

LOST DOG
---- $REWARD

lost on 12/09

Please Call
█.384.3624
█.925.4590

He never left home be...

LOST DOG
REWARD

RED IRISH SETTER
MALE "TYLER"
PLEASE CALL
847█-1931
REWARD $$$

I wish I had just ... him ... close ... morning

LOST PUPPY

"MOLLY"
BLACK STD
POODLE

REWARD

█-5862

I know we ... exchange ...

LOST DOG
QUEENSLAND HEALER
Grey and Black
Tan on chest and feet

"Reba"

Last seen running towards the Garden St
underpass on July 4th.
Please call (805) █-5385
$REWARD$

Being all alo... also much harder th... imagined

LOST CAT

Named: Kiki
Color: White, currently with a short lion hair cut
Breed: Silver Shaded Persian

Reward $200.00

Phone: 7█-531-6688

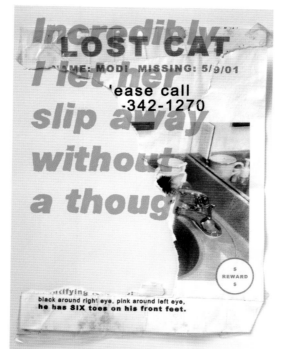

Incredibly I let her slip away without a thoug...

LOST CAT
NAME: MODI MISSING: 5/9/01

...ease call
-342-1270

$ REWARD $

black around right eye, pink around left eye,
he has SIX toes on his front feet.

It should not have ended

LOST BIRD

White Cockatiel

with Yellow - Call

5█████585

if you see it!

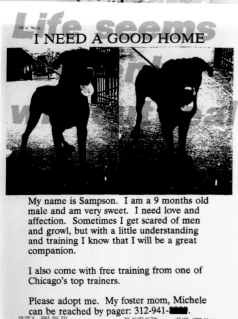

Life seems...

I NEED A GOOD HOME

My name is Sampson. I am a 9 months old male and am very sweet. I need love and affection. Sometimes I get scared of men and growl, but with a little understanding and training I know that I will be a great companion.

I also come with free training from one of Chicago's top trainers.

Please adopt me. My foster mom, Michele can be reached by pager: 312-941-█████.

Who would ever th... to st... lo...

LOST CAT

today's date: 8/21/99

LOST AROUND LEAVITT & MILWAUKEE

NAME: "MOAB"
- gray
- long haired

very friendly

last seen Sun. Aug. 15

(day) 312.███.9635 or 773.███.9822 (night)

PLEASE CALL IF YOU'VE SEEN HER

I'm sure it's all my fault

LOST KITTEN
TIGER-STRIPED
CALICO; FEMA
█████1-3461
downsta...
6799 Trigo

I hope she knows that I'll be here when she comes back

FOUND

Large Black & Tan Dog

On 8/16/00
Near Hermitage & Courtland

Please Page 1█/941-8889

Must Show Proof of Ownership

It's hard to imagine any one else now that he's gone

DOG FOUND

TUESDAY 11/21 7PM ON WEBSTER ST.

BLACK MALE PUPPY WITH WHITE FLEA COLLAR

CALL 773-██2-4509 (H)
or 312-2█-4692 (W)

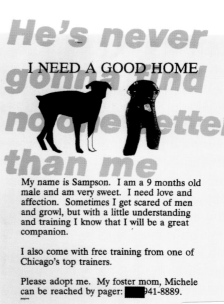

He's never gonna... no one better than me

I NEED A GOOD HOME

My name is Sampson. I am a 9 months old male and am very sweet. I need love and affection. Sometimes I get scared of men and growl, but with a little understanding and training I know that I will be a great companion.

I also come with free training from one of Chicago's top trainers.

Please adopt me. My foster mom, Michele can be reached by pager: █941-8889.

At the beginning of the summer, I hit a dog. It was horrible for everyone involved — the dog especially, the family she is part of, and me — I felt like I'd hit a person. Chester told Rick the story of this accident and the events that followed shortly after it happened. Then I told the story to Rick pretty much as it is written here.

It's the Wednesday night before the 4th, **I'm just off** the 6.01 train from Chicago. This afternoon, a trusted collaborator e-mailed everyone in my office a series of eerily well-retouched images imagining the Sears Tower in the same clouds of smoke and fire New York saw last September — it left us all off-balance and remembering. I have a strong feeling of tension and relief about the holiday, but the long weekend won't really start until **I'm turning into the** winding driveway of the coach house my boyfriend/fiancé* rents. We just got quasi-engaged the night before — that is, we decided to get engaged. I pick up his car from his **office** in downtown Barrington to drive myself home on the first night of our new routine where he'll bike to work and I'll drive into town to catch the morning express train.

I've lived in the city for the past five years. **I moved out** to Barrington in late May — it is my home, but I've got another move ahead in the fall when I start graduate school at Yale. So I live in Barrington, **my life is in Barrington, but most of the time I can't quite tell you what street I'm on** when I'm there. It has been interesting to spend the day in the city and the evening in a suburb that feels like the country. We have a hawk nesting in a huge tree outside the bedroom window. We've seen a newly born fawn sleeping in the yard. We watch a family of groundhogs hop in their strange and nervous ways between the coach house and our landlord's estate — their bodies moving heavily with muscular jerks, like animated sandbags. There is a **confused** bird nearby we've heard singing the exact sequence of beeps our alarm clock makes. It is a strong contrast to the city sounds **I've grown accustomed to** — the buses, car horns, **the late-night** matter-of-fact policeman's voice **shouting** to one of the neighborhood teenaged boys, **"You run, you're done."**

It is the 3rd of July. It's seven o'clock. **I am** in the car, just turned out of the small office/house parking lot. I pass the FedEx truck that I see every day at this time. The street is covered in patches by soft, late-summer shadows. The sun slips through the trees in those Bible-like bands that don't really happen in the city. I see **a fast-moving** black shape and brake at what feels like the same moment as I hear the sound of a thud, a whimper, and nails sliding on pavement. I turn the car off and leave it stopped in front of a white house, hazards on. A **small boy** is **running** down the lawn at a house **across the street,** toward me. I ask him to stay

where he is. I don't want him to run out into the street. I have this **panicked** feeling that he too will be hit if he steps off the sidewalk. He is standing there, darkly tanned in the way only children get, he's wearing blue shorts, sandals, and patches of dirt. A second boy, exactly the same size (a twin?), is coming down the front steps — he's taking them in that little-kid way where they step down with the same foot each time. Step, **stop,** steady, step . . . hand up above his head so he can **hold on** to the railing. Their house is a square wood-frame building, its yellow and red paint job has worn away or maybe has been scraped off to be reapplied. Another huge black dog is standing beside the first boy. "Where is your mom?" I ask him. "Go get your mom, **okay?"**

The dog ran throughout the entire collision. I could hear her moving along the front end of the car until it finally came to a stop. I had been driving under 20 miles an hour, but I felt sure I had killed her. As I got out of the car, I heard her feet continue to skid until she got her bearings and then she ran mindlessly on. I **worried** that the little boy had seen all of this too. After **I was sure** he wouldn't come over, I followed the dog into the backyard of the white house. I drive up and down this street twice a day, **but I don't know anyone** who lives on it. It felt strange but still somehow allowed to walk behind the public faces of the houses and into their private yards. I **looked** low **for** the dog, wondering if she'd run back there to find **a safe place to hide** and die.

My dad hit a dog when I was six — or the dog hit us. She ran down her sloping yard and charged headfirst into the back fender of our Bug. I heard my dad make a sound like he'd been punched when it happened. Afterward, the dog ran to the sidewalk as though it was fine, shook hard, fell, and then died. The owner ran down her lawn toward us, then sat petting the still black dog. She told us kindly that it was okay, that we should go. We cried during the rest of the drive — something that I'd never seen my parents do before and that has never happened since.

I'm assuming that **it's going to be the same** thing this time. I look for the dog in the weeds and groundcover under the long branches in this backyard. I'm surprised when I don't find her. **I walk back into the street and see a woman run out** from behind the yellow and red house. "I just hit your dog," I tell her. "I know. I heard it happen," **she says.** She's wiping her hands on her blue shorts. **"I just left my kids** there all alone with a neighbor I don't even know. We just moved here. **We've been** in this house for a week." She says her mom is on her **way over now. We just** start walking. It is understood that we are going to **look** for the dog **together.** There aren't any fences between the yards, which are mostly small patches of grass ringed by thin trees and edged with railroad ties. We walk up the block through these spaces. The owner, whose name is Susan, is calling for her dog. Stashie. Tash. Natasha. The house next door to the white one where I've left the car has a separate garage in back with a black car parked inside, doors open. I can see dozens of bags of chips in there. A young Asian woman appears, we ask if she's seen the dog. "It ran through here, circled the house twice, and ran off." We cut straight across into the next yard, there's a young guy in a yellow t-shirt working on a small boat. He hasn't seen the dog. "Sorry," he tells us. We are cutting through hedges, trying to double back at points, but we are unable to figure out exactly how we got to where we are. As we squeeze through a thick row of young trees planted in a bed of rocks, Susan stops to look at my feet to see what kind of shoes I'm wearing to make sure I can walk through this. "Okay," she says when she sees the simple, low flip-flops that I have on.

"We got Tashie from a shelter. We loved her right away. She was going to be destroyed because she had rickets real bad." Susan's face is wide open and round — it's framed by soft brown hair that curls in a sort of "mom" style. She's just over five feet tall, I think. She must look very different when she's not so panicked and upset — right now she's all eyes and her skin seems to be pulled tight from stress. I'm calling my fiancé to tell him why I'm late, asking him to call the police and to try to reach an animal hospital, I've been trying to get someone, but they've all left for the weekend by now. I give Susan the phone so she can call her husband, but he's not there, so she has to leave a message. "Stash has been hit. The kids are with mom. Please come home."

"We got her anyway," she tells me, handing me my phone and getting back to her story. "The vet said, 'You sure? It's going to be six hundred bucks to fix her legs up.' We got her. We skipped a car payment and she had the surgery. We got her because we couldn't have kids." Her eyes are considering mine as she tells me these things — looking and seeing with an intensity that is rare, something you don't realize you go most days without as you talk to friends and colleagues, exchanging glances that remember and assume rather than see, something you might not even think about until a moment like this. I don't really ask questions or interrupt, I just try to listen well, it seems like that's what she needs. "The two boys . . ." I do say this, confused . . . "Miracle babies. They came right along after the doctor said they never would. We had two dogs by then. They're our babies too. I'm just glad that my son didn't see you kill the dog. He saw my dad die and was messed up for a whole year." Susan makes an exaggeratedly blank face and then holds her arms out in front in a semiconscious, zombie-ish parody of the boy. At this moment I feel, more

than ever, like the cartoon bad guy — like I should have a handlebar mustache.

We've gone through a lot of yards and then we end up back in front of the yellow t-shirt guy. I ask him about the dog again, confusing him with the young woman who saw Tash. "Nope. Sorry. Still haven't seen her." In the street a group of Susan's neighbors has come out. The man who lives in the white house is looking at my car and scratching his head — I've blocked him in his driveway. A too-tan woman whose face is lined twenty years beyond her actual age is looking very worried, she and her husband ask if they can help us look for the dog. A teenaged girl comes out next, on her way to buy cigarettes, she says she'll look too. She wants to know who the jerk is who hit her. I don't really hear this, I'm on the phone with the police. I see the girl turn to look at me nervously when she learns that I'm the jerk. Susan tells her gently that I've been helpful.

"There she is!" all of us yell as we see a black dog dart out into the middle of the street, nearly getting hit by a red hatchback. The couple in the car beep their horn a few times at the dog who is happily dashing around them, tail curling into a question mark with pleasure. The dog jumps up and down, trying to bite the car, gesturing as if to say "Hi! Hi! Hi . . . hi!" Susan shakes her head. "That's not her," she says. "Tashie doesn't have a tail."

My brother and I never really had pets as kids. We moved a lot, and our parents had pets growing up so must have known from their own kid behavior they'd be the ones doing the caretaking if they got us one. They did make a go with some goldfish one year — we went through several pairs. My brother would name the little transparent fish bizarrely and adamantly. "Rocky. Yep. Rocky," he'd say. Some mornings we'd come downstairs and find the bowl empty except for the plastic branch swaying side to side in the neon rocks next to the tiny castle. "Where are the fish?" we'd want to know. "Um. Gone," our mom would say. There would be tears and worry as we wondered what she had done with the "bodies." Then we'd go through it all again, the clear plastic bag holding two fish, tap water, and three inches of air. "Fred," my brother would say. Or Doug. "That's his name. I'm sure." He'd put his hand up in the air, palm out to push his point home. I think our parents understood the enormity of having a pet — we didn't really get it, and the fish might not have been enough of a lesson. They were lovely and sweet, but kept up away from us in a glass bowl, replaced easily and often, for less than five dollars.

I ask Susan if she would like to go out in my car to look for the dog. This way we can cover more ground. She nods.

We drive very slowly up the street, constantly pulling over, hazards on. People in cars twice the size of mine are flying past us trying to get wherever they're going — fast. We make it up the block and just around the corner. I can tell that Susan wants to be walking again, I think I would too, sitting makes us feel like we're not doing anything. "Here. Stop here," she says. We pull into one of the house/offices — a State Farm branch. "It's okay. We can park it here, he's my insurance guy," Susan tells me, pointing at a wood-carved sign swinging out front with his name on it — Jim Dugan.

"Our old **house was on six acres of land.** Tashie doesn't get it. She's kind of a special dog — scared of everything and not very smart." We're back in the yards again, very close to where we started. **We don't even look for paths anymore,** we just plow through trees and hedges. "She didn't have any tags on — **we just** went to the vet today. She won't **know** where she is," Susan says looking at **the unfamiliarity of her** new neighborhood. My phone is ringing. It's the police. "Ma'am, where are you, ma'am? Your fiancé said you were on Station Street," the dispatcher says. "I know. I was. But we left. We went out in the car to look for the dog," I tell her. "So you're in the car?" "No. We're in someone's yard. We left the car at Jim Dugan's place," I say. I can't remember what street that's on but feel like **that's all I have to say.** "Oh, sure, Jim. He's my insurance guy." This is what I expect to hear — this is what I think happens outside the city, but my idea is only a TV-based one because the dispatcher doesn't know what I'm talking about. "Okay. Just go back there," **she tells me.** "The officers will try to find you.**"

I'm waiting at the car when the police arrive. I feel like a criminal and won't be surprised if they cuff me. "Book her," they'll say. Except this doesn't happen at all. The officers are so nice. **A man and a woman. She's in the driver's seat,** he's wearing cop-show-style silver mirrored sunglasses that he never takes off. The female officer does all the talking. Really, **I do all the talking.** I tell the whole story . . . The city. The train. The blur of the dog. The car full of chips. The yellow t-shirt guy. The neighbors. The question-mark dog. **The kids.** The rickets story. **The miracle babies.** The boy after his grandfather's death — I'm sure I make the same blank face Susan did, **arms out.** Jim Dugan . . . Both officers **smile indulgently** as I ramble. They wait patiently until I trail off. **"Any damage** to the car?**"** they ask. **"No!** None," I tell them. "Then we won't have to file a report," they say. I can tell they're done. "So!?" I want to shout. "The dog . . .?" I start to ask.

"Oh, **she'll probably come back. She just ran off somewhere.** Have a good holiday." The woman pulls out a clipboard and a pen. "You can go. Okay?" She's waiting for me to go so she can start writing. They must have to keep some sort of record about the incident — maybe just for a laugh back at the station about my berserk list of facts. "After she hit the dog, the driver saw a car full of chips . . . ," they'll write. "No damage to either vehicle." I have to somehow get my car around theirs to pull out of the tiny driveway. There's just enough room to turn it around, but I'm driving far more cautiously than I did on my first road test as I circle past them and turn out onto what I now see is Lake Cook Road.

A year or so after the fish, my brother had a pet rabbit for an hour. It was Easter and our parents had taken us to a nice hotel in Denver for a holiday brunch. Just inside the hotel lobby there was a giant chocolate egg towering on a makeshift pedestal. This was surrounded loosely by a low picket fence that corralled dozens of extremely nervous wild rabbits. Parents and children walked in, well dressed in thin fabrics of soft colors, and stopped short at this sight. No one knew what to make of the rabbits — their gamy smell filled the big room, overriding the large and expensive floral arrangements that had been ordered just for this day. No kids ate at this brunch. A group of very small children trailed back and forth between the dining room and the big egg, maybe one would be holding a piece of bacon that was easily dropped and forgotten. All of us were excited **in the special way kids get in the face of a large-scale, adult mistake.** *As the brunch began to wind down, little boys started helping each other scale the fence. All the kids were chasing the rabbits, diving to grab their back legs. Some girls and boys wandered around with their catch pressed against their suit or party dress. "Can we take it home?" All of the families were leaving with a rabbit. Some two. "Oh, yes, please!" the management said.*

My brother appeared before us, sweaty, ragged, and wild-eyed, with a light brown rabbit squirming in his arms — he and the animal looked equally nervous. My **parents** *must have been* **broken in some way** *by the sight because ten minutes later we were all in the car. My brother and I had to try to hold the rabbit down on top of a pile of newspapers, because with every turn, it lurched and clawed, running in place, eyes rolling.* **We rode most of the way home like this,** *my brother and I both* **imagining the reality of** *trying to bring this creature to live at our house. As we passed a nature reserve, our dad slowed the car.* **"How** *about* **we leave** *the little guy here? I think this is his home." My brother jerked the door open and watched in fear and relief as the rabbit hopped over his lap, away. This was when we began to get what it means to have a pet. Seeing the rabbit so far removed from its natural environment,* **so frightened and out of control,** *we could not escape understanding that it would be* **a lot to ask,** **too much** *even,* **to try to** *make it* **live with us. We finally** *understood* what our parents knew, that in a way, if you're doing it right, your pets own you.

Back at Susan's house, there are now a dozen neighbors standing around in the street. Everyone knows what role I've played in the evening's events. I talk to the next-door neighbor for a bit. Her own dog is walking around in her neatly kept fenced yard. "I never let her outside the fence. Never. Sometimes my husband does, though." She whispers this part, annoyed. The dog is perfect and fluffy — like she's bathed every day. She kind of kicks her legs up with each step, which makes her look, absurdly, like she is walking around on pillows back there. Susan's mom walks over to us. Her face is harsh, and her pallor looks gray next to her youthfully lightened hair. Her expression shows me that this kind of thing must happen to her all the time. I tell her what the police have said. **She's plainly angry with me.** She **doesn't think** the dog will be fine. "She probably ran off to die. **They do that, you know.**" She nods her head with each word as punctuation, folds her arms, and turns away.

At this moment, Susan's husband comes home. He drives up in a burgundy minivan. He's wearing blue shorts, sandals, no shirt, and silver mirrored sunglasses that he doesn't take off. He is startled at the sight of all of us and wants to know what's going on — it is clear he has not listened to his phone messages yet. "Your dog was hit by a car," I say. The neighbor I've been talking to starts to back away. "I mean, I hit your dog. It was an accident." As I'm telling him the story, his face is stony. I have no idea how to read him — I can't see his eyes at all. **"Okay,"** he says when **I've told** him **most of the story. "Okay."** His boys have come out of the house, they've been waiting for him, watching from the front window.

"Dad?" the first one says, **"Dad!** The dog was chasing a cat. Then she got hit by a car. And then she ran away. She ran around that house down there, in a circle. Two times!" He's pointing at the potato chip house. **"And then she ran waaay** down there," he says, drawing out the words for emphasis, his high voice getting higher as he points to the end of the block. **"And she turned the corner and I couldn't see her anymore."** This little boy knew more than anyone else. Susan and I were wasting our time looking in the yards, Natasha had run far past our search within minutes of the accident. **"Dad?"** The second little boy steps up, wanting to tell his own version of the story. He speaks slowly in a young high voice that matches his brother's. He's rubbing an eye and raising his other arm up in the air like he wants to ask a question. **"Dad,"** he says, "the dog got hit."

The man picks up both of the boys, one in each arm. "That's why **you** should never run into the street," he tells them.

"You might get hit by a car. **Okay?** So you don't ever do that. You're smarter than that dog."

It's starting to get dark now. The small crowd is breaking up. **Everyone is going home. I leave** my phone number with the neighbor I've talked with the most and ask her to give it to Susan. My fiancé is waiting for me at home, **worried.** I stop the car in front of the garage when I arrive in case he wants to check it for damages. **He doesn't care** about that right now, though, which feels good. He becomes **a huge hug,** then steps away to take the emergency brake off so he can push the small car into the garage. In his **careful and kind** way he is quietly telling me **"It's okay"** and **"No more** cars **for today."**

A few days later there is a message from Susan. Natasha is okay, the police F O U N D her the next morning on the front stoop of her old house, a distance we figure to be about six or seven miles away. She has a bruised kidney and a broken rib. She's sleeping in the kitchen. **She is going to be fine.**

*My uncle Terry had a giant dog, an Airedale named Kid. She was around before **I was** and lived until I was sixteen — that summer she stood taking small steps, waiting impatiently for you to throw the ball even though you just did and it had flown past her milky eyes unnoticed. Kid always wore a bandanna around her neck. She always sat in the front seat of Terry's little MG, his girlfriend had to perch on the narrow shelf in the back. If my uncle stopped for lunch, he always ordered **the same** thing for the dog.*

*I'm told that once Terry tried to leave Kid with his girlfriend for a couple of days. The dog watched my uncle from the window as he walked down the street, she looked at the girl-friend, then again outside, sighed, and took a few steps back to get enough momentum to break right through the low plate glass. Terry turned and saw Kid shaking off the shards like water and took her with him, wherever he was **going**.*

Written by Tracy Jenkins — 2002.09.11. Encrypted by Rick Valicenti — 2003.02.14. Typeset in Nillennium Italic and Nillennium Text, a new member of the Nillennium family by chester _ exclusively Thirstype.com

home
is
where
the ♡
is

We interrupt this program…
Suburban Maul was a meditation on out-of-control branding.
What would happen if this extended to neighborhood homes?
To find out, visit www.emotionaspromotion.com.
(Full disclosure: Fear of litigation prevented reproduction of those images here.)

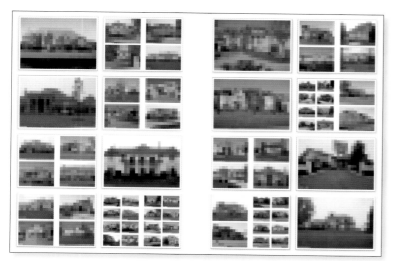

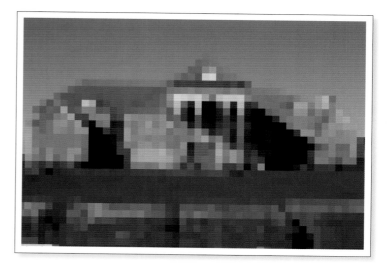

ONETWO

BUSH
2004

oleanna

a play by David Mamet presented in the Black Box Theatre

directed by Sonny Valicenti featuring Dan Andruss and Catherine Davis
22.23.24 April 2004 7:30pm Barrington High School

BUSH

"America the Beautifool."

blind **a**rchangel **w**ar **l**ockstep

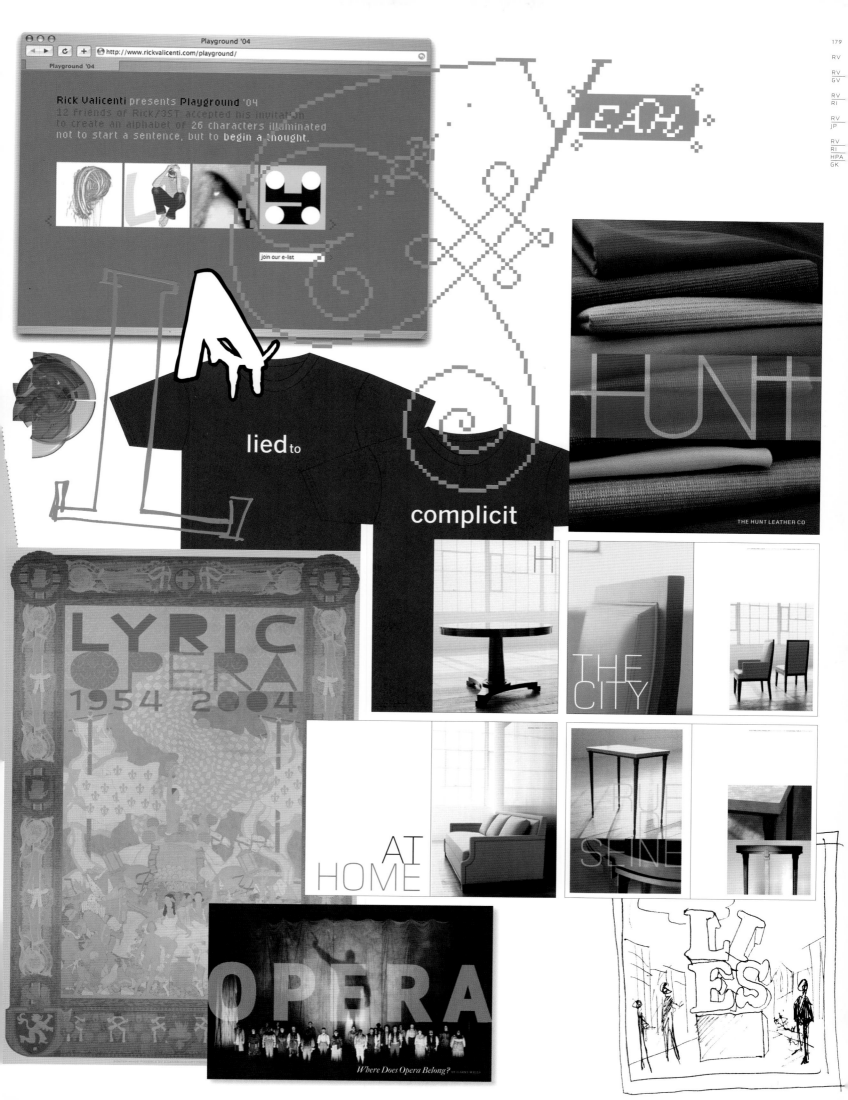

Playground '04

http://www.rickvalicenti.com/playground/

Playground '04

Rick Valicenti presents **Playground** '04

12 friends of Rick/3ST accepted his invitation to create an alphabet of 26 characters illuminated not to start a sentence, but to begin a thought.

join our e-list

lied to

complicit

THE HUNT LEATHER CO

LYRIC OPERA 1954 2004

THE CITY

AT HOME

SEINE

OPERA

Where Does Opera Belong?

Barrington, area (in sq. miles): 6.8 (3,537,438 US)   number of households: 3,767 (105,904,641 US)

median age: 38.6 (35.9 US)   median housing price: $329,900 ($119,600 US)

median household income: $83,085 ($41,994 US)   unemployment rate: 1.9% (3.9% US)

college degree holders: 58% (24.4% US)   caucasian population: 96.2% (75.1% US)

All statistics are from the 2000 US Census.

America the Beautiful
by Robert McAnulty *Robertson+McAnulty Architects*

If you have already flipped through the photographs in this peculiar little folio (as I did) and are now turning to this text for some clue as to its titling, we can only surmise that *maul* must mean something like the activity of malling (were mall to be made a verb...). To mall, then, is *to maul*. Yet as violent an elision as this wordplay suggests, the images are no more than a series of rather familiar examples of what we now call McMansions. FOOTNOTE: McMansion: *noun*. A large, opulent house, especially a new house that has a size and style that doesn't fit in with the surrounding houses... The word *McMansion* has only been a part of the lexicon for a little over ten years, but it has already undergone a fairly significant change in meaning. In fact, the word's current meaning seems to be almost the opposite of its original sense. As the following citation shows... *McMansion* used to mean something similar to *cookie-cutter house* (that is, a house that has a bland style that's identical to all the nearby houses):

> In this dehumanizing, auto-dominated, market-research-driven age of faltering standards of service and aesthetics, our urban and suburban landscapes are becoming more homogenized and worse. What character their history and ecology might offer is being strip-mined to make way for anonymous residential projects, monolithic office towers, climate-controlled retail complexes of questionable design and awkward transportation systems – all in the abused name of progress. We are talking here of the march of mini-malls and 'McMansions.' Sam Hall Kaplan, 'Search for Environmental View of Design,' *The Los Angeles Times*, July 17, 1990.

This fits nicely with the formation of the word, which is *McDonalds* (the fast-food chain) + *mansion*. After all, what could be more bland and 'cookie cutter' than the fare served by McDonalds? www.wordspy.com/words/McMansion.asp. A closer look shows that the familiarity of the images has been subtly (and disturbingly) undermined by Thirst's manipulations. Our curiosity piqued by the insidious banality FOOTNOTE: The

I

---

early films of David Lynch share Thirst's preoccupation with the bizarre underpinnings of everyday experience. 'Beneath the familiar, peaceful, "American-dream" cleanliness of the daytime scenes lurks sleaziness, prostitution, unrestrained violence, and perversity...' Tim Dirks, www.filmsite.org. of these photographs, we still may be wondering how these homes of the newly rich are like malls. And really, even if we were convinced of their mall-ness, why should we care? After all, have we not learned that the mall is the quintessential building type of the late 20th century? Is there a soul left in the country who does not heed the cry 'Shopping is the quintessential experience of late capitalism'? FOOTNOTE: *Harvard Design School Guide to Shopping* (Cologne: Taschen, 2002). Yet we are still faced with the peculiar Thirstian imagery and its ironic inversion of privacy (the home) and publicity (the mall). What are they getting at? What, we might ask, does the mall actually *maul*? Better yet, how does the mall *maul*? And what happens when 'home sweet home' has been *mauled*? FOOTNOTE: In the film *Grosse Point Blank*, John Cusack's character returns to his suburban Michigan 'home' only to find a 'Kwik Mart' in its place. It is a comic scene and only the tip of the iceberg in terms of the refitting of homes in suburban America. In a recent *New York Times* article, Charles Strum describes returning to his childhood home:

> Driving past, I couldn't find it. I stopped and stared, then backed up and stared again. The houses on either side were the same; the one between them was not my house. In its place was a McMansion, a big box squeezed into the original lot and best described as lacking architecture. It felt like a mugging... Of course, that's just my opinion. One man's McMansion is another's castle. Charles Strum, 'Homesick in Suburbia,' *The New York Times*, September 29, 2002.

'Experience the concept of simple abundance unfolding from the winding drive and through whispering pines – revealing the majestic, yet

Following the explosion in personal fortunes that marked the dot.com nineties, a newly wealthy class streamed to the distant suburbs with an eye to building dream homes. Fifty years earlier, the end of WWII had witnessed the first iteration of dream homes in the underdeveloped

II

fields surrounding America's cities. Markets fueled by the return of GIs, the pressure of the automobile industry, and the growth of the federal highway system produced Levittown-like developments FOOTNOTE: Peter Bacon Hales, 'Building Levittown: A Rudimentary Primer,' http://tigger.uic.edu/~pbhales/building.html. full of affordable homes on quarter-acre lots now familiar to us from television shows like *Leave It to Beaver*.

A real estate market driven by postwar economies of scale produced the modesty of the conformist (yet comfortable) cookie-cutter-style 'little boxes' lamented by Joni Mitchell 30 years ago. Conformity was the order of the day for the 'Organization Man' FOOTNOTE: William Whyte, *The Organization Man* (New York: Doubleday, 1956). and his neighbors in the massive developments that reproduced across the landscape like frenzied fungi in an orgy of self-replication. Now, nearly half a century later, the suburbs are still growing, but a mutation is straining the 'scape. An architectural 'sameness' still rules the suburbs, FOOTNOTE: A sentiment with the darkest connotations if one goes back and reads the chilling post-Columbine *New York Times* editorial pages:

> What sense of place can there be in the Littletons of America now, in these mall-lands where each Gap and McDonald's is like the next, where the differences between things are neither prized nor scorned but are simply wiped from existence? Growing up in an anonymous landscape, how can anyone escape his own encroaching sense of anonymity? In this world, meaning evaporates; in a world of monotonous getting and spending, the need to shake things up, to make a mark – any mark – may overpower everything else, including sense. Stephen Schiff, 'Littleton, Then and Now,' *The New York Times*, April 22, 1999.

simple lines of this Colorado-styled residence. Man melds with nature within the 14,000 plus square feet offering 30-foot soaring ceilings and walls of glass.'

but bigness now signifies 'bidness' (as they say in Texas). The newly rich have redefined the very idea of 'home.' The McMansions of the dot.com nineties are much closer to the 'home' of *Martha Stewart Living*,

III

FOOTNOTE: Ms. Stewart's recent legal troubles for her alleged insider trading seem to typify the bloated need to 'consume and conquer' that fueled the economy of the late nineties, and possibly the bulk of these homes. The lack of scale in terms of the 'miraculous' tech stock and dot.com payouts may have bled into the overscaling of these homes and also into territories such as Ms. Stewart's, where the blindness of greed may have led one to risk it all to save less than half (a quarter, perhaps?) of the cost of one of the McMansions featured in this book. the 'home' of Barry Diller's *Home Shopping Network,* Canon's 'home office,' Sony's 'home entertainment center,' the movie *Home Alone III*'s 'smart-home.' Even the site of 'good ol' home sweet home' FOOTNOTE: Which has perhaps been replaced by new governmental programs imploring us to spy on our neighbors. Or has the idea of 'home' worn out its welcome with the perhaps too-repeated W-ism 'da Homeland'? has been dramatically reconfigured. Joni Mitchell's 'paradise' FOOTNOTE: Joni Mitchell. 'Big Yellow Taxi,' from *Ladies of the Canyon*, 1970. continues to be replaced by parking lots, but now the parking lots have engulfed the home. The lawns of the late 20th century are more like tiny putting greens than unruly fields of grass, isolated islands in an automotive landscape heated from below to prevent icing. Even the annoying goose shit is vacuumed off the green carpets on a regular basis.

Maul samples sixty-nine of these new 'homes' with the irony that has become the trademark of Thirst, a small band of itinerant visionaires who have long been working on the outskirts of design practice. *Maul*'s photographs bear witness to the plight of recently rural areas throughout the United States. The homes it shows dot Barrington, Illinois, once an oceanlike field of prairie grasses just north of Chicago's O'Hare airport. But don't be fooled: *Maul*'s insistent irony masks a serious critique. Barrington is Thirst's home, FOOTNOTE: Thirst's office sits on a quiet residential street in 'downtown' Barrington. It is a quick walk to the large grocery store or Starbucks – both are within eyeshot of the building. Soon there will be a new condominium/mall structure just down the street

that will feature the 'best' in high-end shopping and living. and *Maul* is nothing less than a desperate attempt by these designers to 'exorcise the demons' hidden beyond the facades of these insidious invaders.

So what's up with these photos (signage notwithstanding)? Sixty-nine homes, all built for the entrepreneurial class that was spawned by the 'new economy.' Some of the brightest, most inventive minds in the world are trapped in these homes. Here – the inventor of the IPO, there – the venture capitalist who risked backing Amazon… Inventors, risk-takers, business mavericks – these are hardly the conformists of the Eisenhower years. Why, then, do their homes look so similar? Why have architects and designers failed so miserably to transform the historical and material codes of the rural Midwest into something more inventive than 'French Provincial' and 'Georgian'? While we may deplore the repetitive banality of our Levittowns, it is the repetitive grandiosity of our newly minted McMansions that is even more troubling. FOOTNOTE: A bit more from *The Times*… *In place of genteel white clapboard or ivy-covered brick on plots with wide side yards, houses of mocha stone or battleship gray stucco now predominate. Scale is ignored. The design features are all too familiar: neoclassic garage doors competing for prominence with colonnaded entryways, or the blind stare of several sets of over-size windows. Nearly windowless side walls face each other like warehouses across an alley. The new houses appear to be mutations in the evolution of the American home.* Charles Strum, 'Homesick in Suburbia,' *The New York Times*, September 29, 2002.

'As you pass through the coach-lit, stone column, gated entry down the tree-lined winding drive you ask yourself am I in *Wynstone*, or Nantucket, or the Carolinas?'

A closer look at the photographs sheds a quirky light on these questions. Sixty-nine (a curious number…) photos: 69 homes – all purposely shot without any of the realtor's predilection for comforting imagery. There are no swimming pools, no families (no bodies whatsoever), only 69 huge

IV

V

---

homes, 13 cars, a few recently planted trees, lots of discreet bushes, and acres of smooth pavement. The images are symmetrically photographed like the McMansions they depict (which are almost always bilaterally symmetrical). Symmetry is just cheaper to build – one half of the house is simply a carbon copy of itself. Such mirroring has deep connections to the classical European models endorsed by historicist postmodernism. FOOTNOTE: Chicago continues to be condemned to lip-synching the neotraditionalist tunes begun by the Chicago Seven (led by the ubiquitous Stanley Tigerman) in the late 1970s.

Although the architectural community bears responsibility for endorsing the historicist impulse (as a critique of modernism's formal excesses), the sad fact of the matter is that most McMansions are kit homes built by developers from preexisting plans. These homes are enormous, often as large as 10,000 square feet (vs. the Levittown homes of 2,000 square feet). They almost always feature a Palladian window – borrowed from Andrea Palladio's orderly 16th-century designs for the landed Italian gentry (famously knocked off in the U.S. by Thomas Jefferson). Steeply gabled roofs abound – the more the merrier. Turrets signify the sought-after 'starter castle' look even more bluntly. Whatever their cosmetic differences (and there are many), these bloated buildings all run together by virtue of the enormity of their scale. Certainly these homes represent the repudiation of the old functionalist dictum 'form follows function.' After all, what family's function could possibly require such monstrous form? FOOTNOTE: Other than MTV's *The Osbournes.* Thirst has an idea…

In the eyes of the Thirstees, the dot.com nineties ended quite abruptly on September 11th and the sheen has quickly worn off the nation's economic apple. Many newly rich Generation Xers face the necessity of liquefying their only real assets – real estate holdings have gone on the

block. Foreclosures loom as banks fold. FOOTNOTE: A brand new McMansion just down the street from one Thirst employee has very recently gone on the market because its owners are now unable to cover its property taxes. *Maul* has set up the question for us: in a declining economy, what is to become of these huge homelike constructions that blot Barrington's landscape like so many enormous fossils? A clue to the answer is found in the manipulations of the images – in short, the houses have been 'shopped' with signs. FOOTNOTE: In addition to the more obvious relationship to shopping, I refer here to the digital manipulations of the photographs done with the aid of the software program Adobe Photoshop. What is remarkable is how simple it is to transform our reading of these buildings from bloated McMansions to corporate headquarters – simply by the application of the corporate signage. The appliqué is familiar to us as the advertising imagery of the corporate brand. 'Branding' is a buzzword that has not only survived the economic downturn but been energized by shrinking markets. 'Everybody loves branding: we embrace it, we consume it, we wear it, we lust for it, some have even killed for it.' FOOTNOTE: Rick Valicenti, in an e-mail message dated 11.05.02. Thirst has, in effect, 'branded' these images – and their branding signage whimsically undermines the McMansion's cravenly classist underpinnings. We are transported to the magical world of shopping – a world where we are invited to let our fantasies run free. We can imagine ourselves as Gap models: lean, hard, and ready to prance. Our sense of self is reflected in our sense of style. We become what we buy, we live the brand experience, we identify with the brand message. In fact, we are branded by brands – we become one with them. And it is all so painless. What would be so wrong with turning the McMansions back over to commerce? FOOTNOTE: One powerful American brand has made recent headlines for clearing its shelves of 'laddie' magazines. *'I really don't want the experience of looking at a Maxim cover and shopping with*

VI

VII

my 2-year-old for a Wiggly Worm to be the same,' said one creeped-out dad. Maureen Dowd, 'Look Good, Act Cool,' *The New York Times*, May 11, 2003. And why is Wal-Mart such an all-star in American branding? *Wal-Mart is not only the world's largest retailer; it is also the most admired company in America, according to Fortune Magazine. It also has a very strong and clearly defined brand identity. Wal-Mart projects itself as the epitome of decent middle-American values . . . [It] has worked hard to nurture a small-town image. And the key to small-town life is that you really don't want to offend people because you have to live with these same people year after year, decade after decade.* David Brooks, 'No Sex Magazines, Please, We're Wal-Mart Shoppers,' *The New York Times*, May 11, 2003.

'Whether you want to entertain on a grand scale or just enjoy family fun on your own compound, this property truly has it all.'

In Thirst's ironic manipulations of the status quo, some may find a certain ambivalence in what seems to be a celebration of the transformative power of the brand. But I think such a reading misses the genuinely subversive element in Thirst's work. We can return to the original wordplay: *maul/mall.* Clearly these monstrous homes maul the landscape with the elimination of any vestige of its natural history, replacing it instead with the remnants of an idealized Euro-past. These overscaled homes become distinguishable only by the application of their branding signage. Without a literal 'brand,' the homes run together like so many pink elephants. This is the Thirst insight: the brand defines the home, not the owner. Some will find this an exciting market to exploit, others will find Thirst's photographs a cynical commentary on creeping commercialism. FOOTNOTE: *I don't know if it strikes you as odd that of all the arenas of human endeavor, the one that has produced the best-selling computer game of all time [the Sims] is the American suburb.* David Brooks, 'Oversimulated Suburbia,' *The New York Times*, November 24, 2002. I prefer to read them as an attempt to 'exorcise the demons well in advance,' FOOTNOTE: Rick V's e-mail. a celebration of heterogeneity and a call for sympathetic invention.

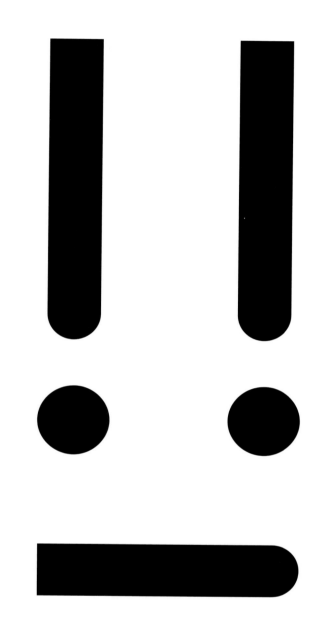

SEX 2075_ ILLUSTRATION FOR *WIRED* "MILLENNIUM" ISSUE WITH CONCEPT SKETCH _2000

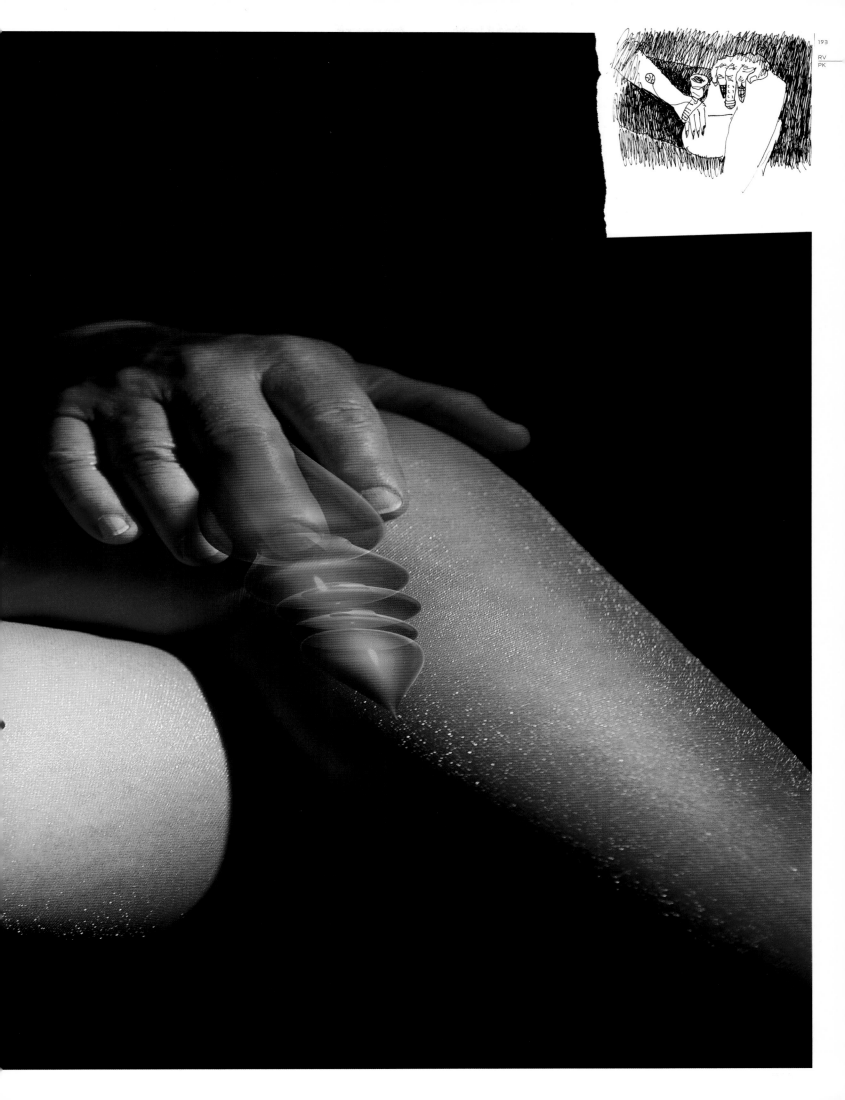

what a difference a button makes!

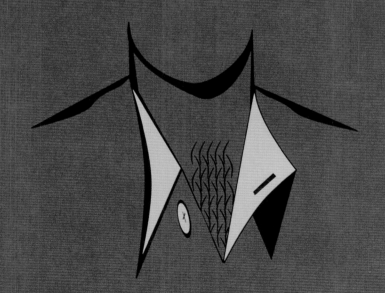

The infamous Marvin Scott Jarrett did indeed place a call to Thirst. I suppose he needed to acknowledge all of the usual design suspects of the time with his "no money" pledge softened by the lure of being the next David Carson.

On this occasion, he called to invite us to create the media kit for *RayGun* magazine: "You know, something that will make a statement and inform the advertisers of our page rates and identify our demographic in relation to their products."

So I pitched, using existing imagery from our cynical period, for an eight-panel, two-sided accordion sheet that would be housed in one of those very hip clear plastic envelopes along with an easily modified sheet of the most current space rates.

I was informed of his enthusiastic caution — which requested a prototype to eliminate the caution. I couldn't imagine David being required to make a prototype — but, whatever — the truth of the matter was that Marvin's budget of next-to-nothing did not include the effort of a prototype, so it was simply better to just make it all happen and run the risk that we would wind up owning the idea and the imagery.

The sculptures had existed in my studio prior to his call so there was no expense there. The photography, however, was created for this specific purpose. Patric enlisted some of his friends, two models were hired, and chester was cast as Jesus.

Outtakes were forwarded to Marvin along with printing specifications, costs, and schedules. No response. Ultimately, my impatience got the better of me and I called…only to learn that the idea was rejected.

Oh well. Life in the fast lane ain't all it's cracked up to be. A few months later, we published our work for ourselves under the title *Want*.

SEDUCE ME

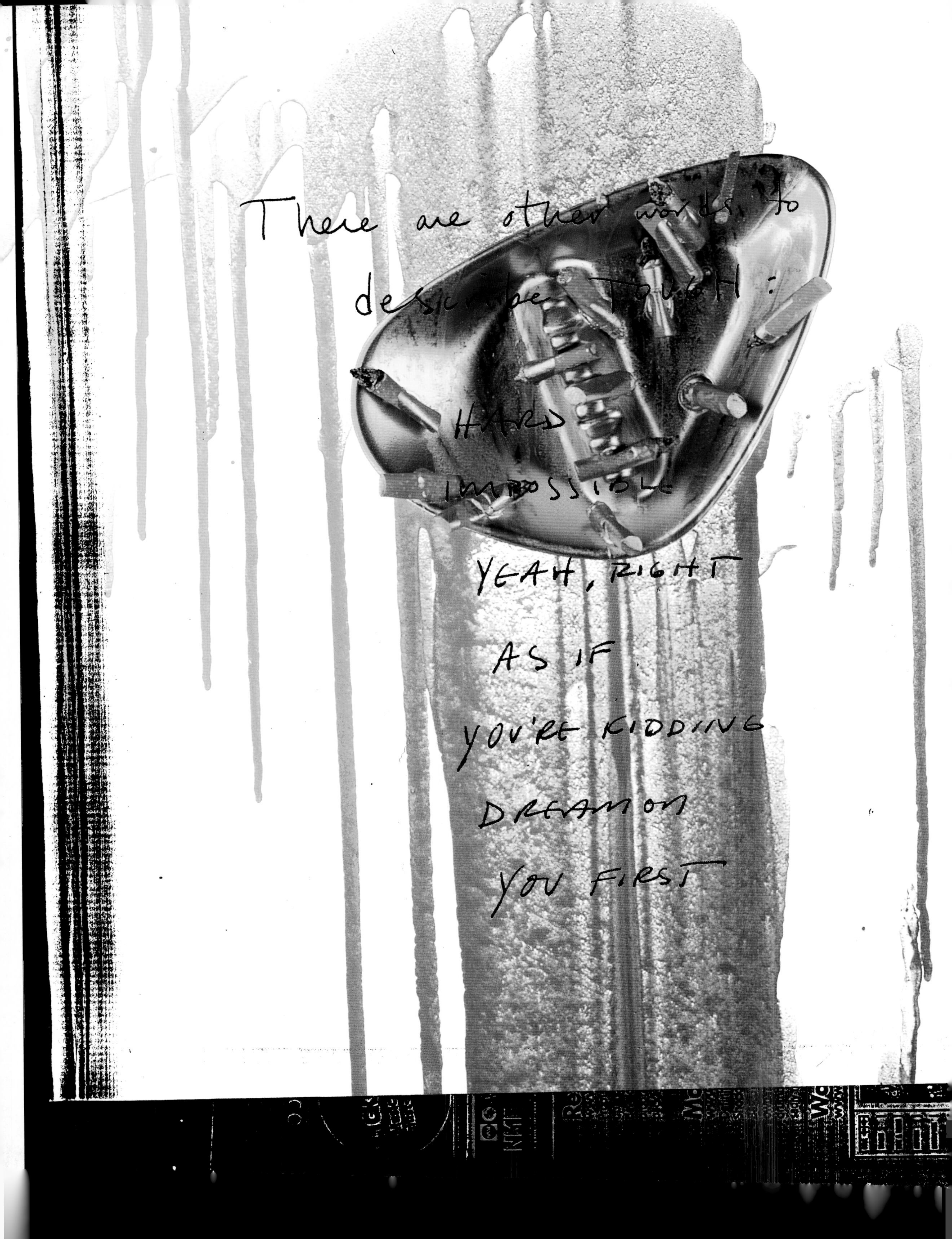

There are other words to
describe Touch:

HARD

IMPOSSIBLE

YEAH, RIGHT

AS IF

YOU'RE KIDDING

DREAM ON

YOU FIRST

NEED ME

I always loved
the facial contortions
in porno flicks.
I vowed never too ~~used~~
watch these damn things
anymore except they
always ~~give me a woody~~.
— gets me soggy.

REPLACE ME

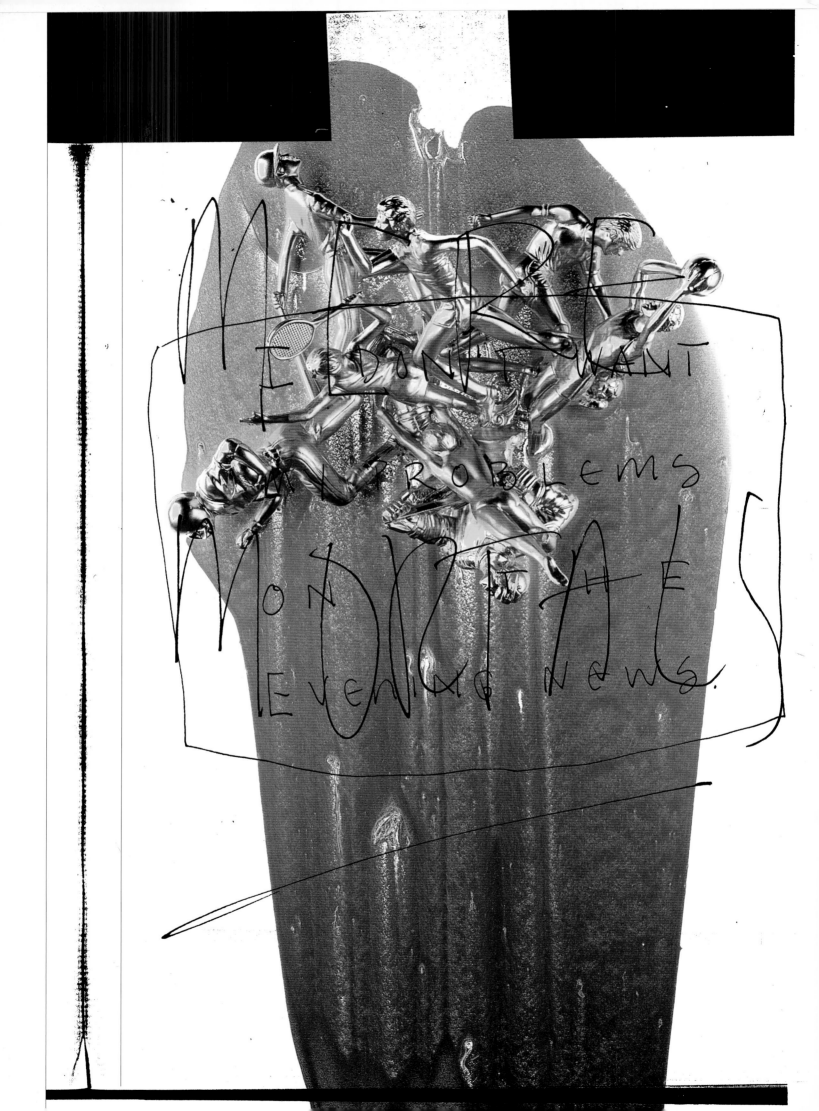

So *I live a normal normal normal and ever so boring life*, and I want you to know that going into this, so that we may at the very beginning of our relationship be just unbelievably honest and horrifyingly deeply into each others' heads in a way that only Dionne's employees can know, and I want you to know that I normally do not act in a way that others would consider publicly unacceptable, but there are certain things that can drive me truly bananas, truly over the edge. Kinda like when all the candy bars on the drool shelf at the checkout in the minimart are all old and crusty. That makes me crazy.

So innyhoo, I'm all getting home from work and I'm doing voicemail and petting the cat who is, as per usual, acting as if I've been gone for six years on crusade to free the Holy Land and have forgotten his kibble. And I'm doing all the usual getting home from work stuff. Whatever. So there's this way-too-excited voicemail from Kirby, who is this guy I share a cubicle with at work.

Kirby is of the clear-nail-polish-and-subtle-scent school of manhood, if you know what I mean. Totally takes care of himself above and beyond, but somehow manages to achieve that rugged man-of-action look that is so important to one's marketability. He is, however, woefully drawn to those of his own sex, and can I say what a waste it is to see people with that much TVQ not propagating? Really tragic to be sure.

So anyway, Kirby's my bud and we do bud things together like laying out of work together to catch the new Bridget Fonda flick, hanging out at the shopeteria and talking about boys in the food court (both of us are sadly unattached at the moment), making foolish purchases, and the like. *You know*: buds.

Anyway, where was I? Yeah. So Kirby's all leaving this freako message on my service, only he's calling from his bathroom — I can tell because he's got this weird little phone by the john that picks up every possible sound and I'm like, "Hell-oh, don't call me while you're peeing, pleeease." So he's all babbling about this new game show that he found on Telemundo, of all places. And I replay the message and I'm all, "¿Telemundo? ¿Que?"

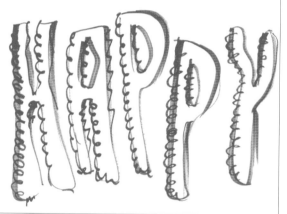

FIGS. 1 & 2

Like what's Kirby doing watching Tex-Mex TV anyway? So, whatever. I call him.

Kirby immediately FREAKS OUT over this new show, of which I have never in my life heard (and that is strange because I experienced the pits of broken-hearted woe last summer and watched the tube religiously for seven days straight and know daytime programming like a broker knows opening time on the floors), and he's all like, "Ohgodohgodohgod you've GOT to come over tomorrow night and we'll watch." And I'm like, "Okaywhateverremindmebye." And he's all, "Bye," and so we hang up and I forget about the entire scenario. (He freaks way too often and way too graphically for the average viewing public. Total TV 14. Not nice at all.)

So it's the last Friday of the month and that is traditionally my get-down-wif-yo-bad-self night, during which I put on the most horrible trashy do-me-with-my-stilettos-in-the-air-and-I-don't-care dress I can possibly conjure up (there is a hideous little place near my house where you can find perilously short dresses for four bucks, which are guaranteed to rip right off at the slightest breeze, and you know it's not a first date thing — I'll write it down for you) and go out to this cool drum-and-bass night at my fave nightclub (so hot, sweaty, and primitive) and shake my little aerobicized butt all night. In light of this eagerly anticipated miniseries of a night, I was not paying any attention to Kirby and his televisual rantings in the least. I forget about the Telemundo invite thing almost immediately.

F I G . 3

I have places to go and men to taunt, and I have no valuable storage RAM to waste on details like Hispanic boobtube soirées with men who are not into me as an object. It's THAT kind of night, you know?

So later that night I show **my** lovely self to the world at the club where I always get in for free (**my** ammunition: the desperate doorguy who wants to take **me** home and bind **my** feet or something) and I parade past the jealous eyes of wannabes and steamy lovers who must stand in line and age while I spend **my** youth in hours of laughter, wine, and joy. So hard to be them, yes? I love it. This is sort of **my** revenge for being a telemarketer; this fabulous little body of **mine** totally works as a weapon. You gotta get one for yourself. Just kidding.

So this place is called Rust, and the decor is…guess what: rust. Duh. And as a place, it's not at all conducive to sitting and chatting; you'd ruin whatever you might be wearing. It's more of a get-up-and-shake-that-groove-thang sort of hole where the music is just that hip, the drinks are just that strong, and the guys are just that buff. Like when you see a nightclub scene in an awful Tommy Lee Jones movie set in the post-apocalyptic near future, and it starts with the line *"In a world gone mad…"* Actually, now that I come to think of it, it's just like the club in that movie, you know, that awful one where Juliette Whatshername is all wearing chain mail and acting rock star and looking all beat up and on heroin…I hate **her so** much.

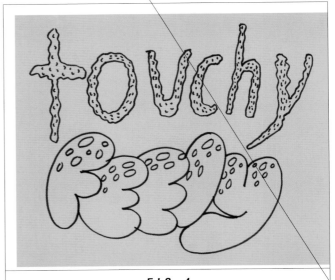

F I G . 4

So I'm all at Rust and I'm having an absolute field day and I'm dancing and I'm drunk and who should walk in with this GORGEOUS man on his arm but Kirby and he's all looking like he just smelled something really bad and he sees me waving like a damned fool and he dumps the hunk right there in the middle of the entryway and very nearly sprints over to me and he's all like, "Horror date. Please save me," and plants a big one right on me so that his glam hunk will see and get the drift that there is no action for him tonight.

Yech. Lips not meant for me and they're all over my face. The celebratory ambience I had been enjoying is gone, and I am put into an abysmal mood. So I punch Kirby and storm off. Color me Krystle Carrington.

I sleep like the dead and wake up at about two in the afternoon and I'm all **"Ohmigod"** and settle down at the kitchen table to write some postcards to friends I haven't talked to in forever, do some coffee and bagels, and before I can say **"boo"** it's seven p.m. — time to hop aboard the weekly prime-time roller coaster.

FIGS. 5 & 6

So I'm really really bored and scanning the boobtube for potential nuggets of entertainment (anything **not** involving overworked syndicated sitcoms) and my eyes are glazing over with hypnosis because I've done a full three laps over the entire bandwidth and I'm perturbed to the point of immediate and irrational purchase of one of those satellite direct systems, like CAN I *PLEASE* HAVE FORTY MORE CHANNELS OF UTTER DRIVEL?

And then I touch down on this weird Mexican station that evidently beams in from planet Tecate when the sun isn't

ABSOLUTART.

FIG. 7

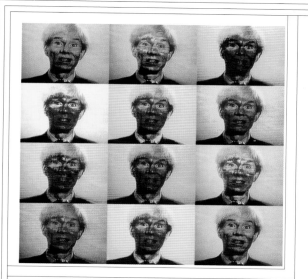

F I G . 8

emitting solar flares, or whatever, because I have never seen it before in my life and I AM UTTERLY MESMERIZED because this is that game show thing that Kirby's been babbling about and can I just tell you it's the weirdest, most reality-proof event I have ever seen (excluding Beverly Hell 90666, I mean). I've dropped right into the middle of this totally life-threatening game show, where paunchy factory workers and horsey housewives are invited to risk life and limb for Mega$$$ (or pesetas, or whatever…) and there I am watching this pudgy little creature of indeterminate gender waving to the cheering (jeering?) audience while being strapped into a safety harness because s/he is evidently going to be hurled AND I DO MEAN HURLED via pulley system (powered by nothing more than celebrity libido from what I can tell) across this flaming lake of Sterno to bust through a brick wall and reach the grand prize, which is a black shiny expensive $edan, shown on a separate stage being flourished and fluffed by a wall of hormonally supercharged Mexican supermodel flesh that is voguing for and seeking validation from the camera eye, which really isn't interested in them at all, for they are teeveeland furniture, and I'm like, "¿a black shiny expensive $edan is worth third-degree burns?" And judging by current televised events, it certainly is SOMEWHERE in the world. So I'm watchingwatchingwatching and I'm amazed that not only is pudgy humanoid being tossed into fate's clumsy hands during prime family viewing time with the addition of a live studio audience, but said audience is SCREAMING FOR PUDGY HUMANOID'S DEATH, and with that my creeped-out-by-the-ferocity-of-human-malaise index redlines, and my spirit is now officially defeated.

F I G . 9

But I am a proud American, so I cannot let my remote control stray from the Truth. Besides, this is just beyond droolworthy, and not only do I turn up the volume, but I speed-dial my old friend Marcus (who is a scrap metal sculptor in Santa Monica) and my old roommate Amanda from college (who is now leading this movie-of-the-week life as a Percodan-addicted bank teller in New York City) and both of them are as completely pop-addled as I am, so I know they'll groove very hard on this. So there we are ON CONFERENCE CALL MIND YOU watching pudgy humanoid reeling toward his/her eventual reward/death and being cheered on by an impenetrable wall of supermodel booty wearing gold wet-look neoprene swimwear and threatening to get it on at any moment, and we are silent over the phone (this conference-call-during-prime-time thing is a normal event among my friends, and I am positive the phone company looooves me to pieces for it) trying to comprehend this sicko show and horrified at its implicit danger and I'm like, "AM I THE ONLY ONE WHO THINKS THIS IS SOOOOOOOOO BEYOND VULGAR?" and the audience roars its answer at me and I am frightened at the guttural sound of their

FIGS. 10 & 11

response. Then all of a sudden, pudgy humanoid, who has been visibly struggling with his/her pulley system (much to the cameraperson's delight), FALLS and I mean really plummets into the fire below and screams the most pathetic scream I've ever heard, and it sounds like

"I've given all my money and my pride for this dream of well-being and would someone please explain it to me because I never quite understood and now I don't have another chance to try," and everyone gasps and then it's silent and it's like all the air has been sucked out of the studio because the flames kind of flare down a little and one of the supermodels starts crying because she doesn't know what else to do and hides her face in a male supermodel's sticky nest of

FIG. 12

hair and then that supermodel freaks out at being put in a position of support like who would he be to know anything about responsibility he's just a supermodel but he knows he should really do something to comfort his coworker but he doesn't know exactly what and so he just stands there shivering in his gold wet-look neoprene bikini then the audience starts to growl because they have been denied the excitement of a full round of game playing and then everyone starts screaming and there are more crying supermodels as a fire squad slowly works its way into the smoldering arena (cables and lights visible for the first time on network television) and they retrieve the smoking body from the once fiery river and all of a sudden it's the Middle Ages again and there's all the evidence of civilization you could want but something's gone so horribly awry that we're all wild again and we don't know how to get away from death and I realize we're still on conference call and I'm sniveling and Marcus and Amanda are likewise losing it and I say "I gotta go" and hang up and I don't understand this tragedy at all and can't someone call pudgy humanoid's

FIG. 13

family and say "I'm sorry things turned out this way, but we can promise you it'll never happen again and here's your black shiny expensive $edan because your spouse won it fair and square." So I go to bed and hide under the sheets, and I wonder if anyone has ever won the car before...

Bling Bling

With its Tiffany-blue background and diamond settings on steroids, this image, originally created for *ESPN* magazine, was a suburban white male's version of the pixel pusher/gangsta aesthetic.
It should be noted that the art director chose to use, as a full-bleed spread, only the area indicated.

Date: Wed, 03 May 2000 16:34:54 -0600

From: Katherine Spring @ a/c/e

Subject: Re: Hi Guys
To: rick@3st2.com, rob@3st2.com, chester@3st2.com

We just got word from our lawyers that ace is fine as a name, but we will have to make a change to the design (so sorry!!!). Here's the deal. Rather than ace reading horizontally with the tagline below it, they'd like ace to be up and down (vertically) with the words that the letters stand for reading across. Sort of like:
alliance
cbot
eurex.
I know this really breaks up the integrity of your design. I apologize. Maintaining as much of the original design/color/ font, etc., as you can, can you guys come up with a look and post it on the site so we can see it?
Please feel free to call and discuss.

Date: Wed, 03 May 2000 23:51:20 -0600

From: chester@3st2.com

Subject: Re: Hi Guys
To: Katherine Spring @ a/c/e
CC: rick@3st2.com, rob@3st2.com

Katie,
This is really quite upsetting news.
And disappointing.

It's kind of amazing to think that a change to "restaurant writing" is a legal recommendation.

I haven't had the chance to speak with Rick about this yet
(he was out of town all day)
but I can only imagine how disappointed he will be.

Rick (and I) are always upset when decisions are driven by the worst possible reasons.
A solution that is not a solution so much as a settlement always looks it, and never stands the test of time.

I hate to be the one to break this news to him.

Yours with head hung somewhat,
chester
Thirst

COUPON

Hello.
My name is:

_____

My best
e-mail address is :

I understand it is my privilege, as the owner of this book, to redeem this original coupon for a complimentary font of the Thirstype type family called Infinity.

I understand that a full collection of Infinity fonts would cost me $150.00 US if I were to purchase it online at www.thirstype.com, which is the web home of Thirstype, Infinity's exclusive distributor. I further understand that this coupon, which offers a free gift worth more than twice as much as the cover price of its enclosing book, must entail a "catch."

I understand that the "catch" entailed by this coupon is not really all that surprising, and is explicated in the following sentence. I understand that I may receive my complimentary font only by removing, in full accordance with the dotted line, and redeeming the original coupon found within the book Emotion As Promotion. I understand that I may not under any circumstances expect or hope to receive a font by substituting for the meticulous removal and redemption of the original coupon one of the following spurious procedures: 1] filling out and mailing, faxing, uploading, dropping in to say hello with, or otherwise transmitting to Thirstype a facsimile of the original coupon; 2] transmitting to Thirstype in any way an original copy of the book Emotion As Promotion with an accompanying note that contains the appeal, or a variation of the appeal, "Hello Thirstype. I am a librarian/bibliophile/historian/ collector/(friend of) the author Nicholson Baker. I could not bring myself to deface my original book, but I would still like to take advantage of your amazing offer. Accompanying this note is my actual book to prove that I own it. Please send a copy of the Infinity typeface to me, and use the enclosed twenty dollars to defray any costs incurred in order to return this book to me in its present

totally pristine condition.
Thank you, please keep the change
for your trouble"; 3] sending material of your own
design that responds to the original coupon's clear "to clip or
not to clip" quandary by attempting to subvert, avoid, or otherwise act
to redeem this offer without actually cutting this page.

I understand, in other words, that I must actually mar a rather costly book if I would like to order my free gift.

I penultimately understand that it is probably in the best interests of 1] the designers of Infinity; 2] Infinity distributor Thirstype; 3] the publisher of Emotion As Promotion; 4] the bookseller; 5] libraries; 6] historians; 7] collectors; and 8] private book-lenders to require for gift font receipt, in addition to a properly filled-out original coupon, the original purchase receipt for my copy of Emotion As Promotion. I understand and appreciate that the above guidelines, without a corollary receipt requirement, only activate the temptation to "poach" whole copies of — or pages containing original gift coupons from — store or library copies of Emotion As Promotion. However, a store receipt will not be required for coupon redemption.

Finally, I understand that failure to have read or understood the above text will not affect my receipt of the full Infinity type family as long as I have 1] filled out this original coupon completely; 2] carefully cut my coupon along the dotted line; and 3] signed my name on the line below.

✗ _____

Infinity® from Thirstype™
This offer never expires.™

Please direct only your completely filled-out, cut-out, original coupons to the following: Typemaster / Thirstype, Inc. / 117 South Cook Street #333 / Barrington, Illinois 60010 / USA

alliance/cbot/eurex

 (proprietary custom typeface)

aBCDeFGHIJKLMNOPQrstUVWXYZ

aBCDeFGHIJKLMNOPQrstUVWXYZ

unicace (based on infotext by erik spiekermann, published by fontshop)

abcDeFGHIJKLMNOPQrstUVWXYZ
0123456789/&$¥£€

Date: Fri, 01 Dec 2000 11:22:40 -0600

From: rick@3st2.com

Subject: ?
To: Stephanie Hammer @ a/c/e

s

your long-term silence is a concern.
pls. advise.

r

Date: Tue, 05 Dec 2000 15:44:13 +0100

From: Stephanie Hammer @ a/c/e

Subject: Antwort: from rick v/thirst
To: rick@3st2.com

r

my long-term silence stems not from my unhappiness
with your work. we are all a bit up in the air concerning
how to proceed with a/c/e. as i am sure you are aware,
some changes (staff-wise) have occurred, which we all
hope will get us back on track. i have spoken with amy
this morning and i will today give the approval for your
bills to be settled. i am pretty disappointed that after
all of our work we really aren't using very much of it...

s

After seven years of producing award-winning corporate communications, the Chicago Board of Trade gave its 1996 annual report business to Thirst, a studio that had never designed an annual report in its life.

Remember Thirst? The bastard child of Lester Beall's Dumbarton Farm and Andy Warhol's Factory? This graphic design collective led by Rick Valicenti is considered by many to be iconoclastic, imposing its esthetic on hapless clients. The reality is somewhat more complex. True, Thirst often uses archetypal imagery, loose wordplay, digital illustration and collage—a form that is seductive to some, horrifying to others. But there is no personal style, Valicenti insists. Just honesty. The work is honest to the "artful process" through which it evolves, honest to the values of its makers. Thirst embraces provocation to gain attention, communicate, and instigate change. And Valicenti accepts himself for what he is: a middle-class surrealist who has taken a lot of heat from his peers for preaching from the sidelines of the field.

By the mid-1990s, after two decades of practice and considerable success, Valicenti began to wonder whether his work had become irrelevant. It became clear to him that no mass audience existed for sophisticated graphic design. In his 1995 manifesto "Backword," he warned his peers to "remember that only the warm, fuzzy, and familiar can serve your effort to communicate any messages of real value."

With a deep sense of relief, he led Thirst out of its home base of Chicago and into the woods 40 miles away. In a picturesque house on 6½ acres, Thirst continues to interweave studio, family, and friends. The community includes Valicenti's wife, Linda; sister, Barbara; brother, William (known typographically as Wm.), and collaborators Patrick King and Chester (no surname).

Valicenti went even farther. He let go of the work he didn't believe in, resigning a number of substantial clients. He can now be intimately involved with the details of every project, as part of a loose and relaxed creative process.

Enter the Chicago Board of Trade. The world's leading futures and options exchange, it had broken its own world volume record in 1996. However, the CBOT faced tough competition from new foreign exchanges. It hoped to meet that competition by increasing operational efficiency, creating new products, and penetrating new markets.

As part of these efforts, the CBOT planned a state-of-the-art $182-million trading floor whose opening became the centerpiece of its 1996 annual report. The catch was that the book had to be delivered one week after the opening. According to vice president of communications Richard Myers, the CBOT wasn't "looking for the firm with the most annual report experience; we were looking for the firm that could do the best job on our annual report."

Long contributing to Valicenti's success has been his ability to engage his clients in the design process. What's more, he thrives on the challenge of working with new and unusual collaborators. He promised to meet the tight production schedule and to stay within a "rather modest" budget

GET OUT OF THE WAY

Thirst does its first annual report.

By Rob Dewey

(neither he nor the client would disclose it). Above all, he convinced the CBOT that Thirst would get out of the way, so that the book would reflect the client's culture rather than his own.

Turning Up the Volume behaves more like a yearbook than a traditional annual report. Its primary function is to reward, through the recording and summation of achievement, members of the exchange who spend $700,000 or more to obtain their seats; CBOT executives and directors; and regulators, including U.S. senators and congressmen. Thirst chose to reflect the story from the audience's point of view.

The process started with interviews with important members of the book's constituency and a review of major events of the past year. Statements arising from that process were dumped into a Quark XPress file and output as spreads to be used as discussion documents. The loosely structured flow suggested an architecture for the piece as a whole, which is linear but somewhat disjointed. This annual report is made up of clearly functional sections, but the section breaks are neither labeled nor self-evident. The effect is something like channel-surfing without the chaos.

The typefaces for this book of the moment were custom-designed by Chester, and by New York designer Barry Deck. (The fonts are now exclusively available through Thirstype.) Its story is told through ephemeral media, such as newspaper photographs and unstyled office shots. The report of a Nobel Prize–winning economist, Merton Miller, is presented as a bound-in letter.

To capture the opening of the CBOT's new trading floor, Thirst commissioned two photographers, Wm. Valicenti and Pulitzer Prize–winning photojournalist Eddie Adams, and executed a carefully planned strategy for documenting the day's events. Runners delivered film to the lab throughout the day. Images were selected, sized, and cropped from the hotel lobby to the color separator, and the finished book was printed and delivered, as promised, within a week.

Thirst's combination of rigorous method and spirited tomfoolery has welded content to context. The book describes the CBOT as powerful, innovative, and sophisticated. Those familiar with Thirst's penchant for hidden messages won't be disappointed—on the spine, for example, is an unlabeled stacked bar chart of the CBOT's 1996 financial results. Nor will they fail to appreciate the exquisite production values.

What's next for Thirst? After the success of the 1996 annual report, CBOT awarded them the project for two more years. As of this writing, Valicenti has just finished directing a 10-second animated TV spot for McDonald's via Leo Burnett. Thirst is also working on the 1997 Gary Fisher Bicycles catalog, putting the finishing touches on the premiere issue of ****, a quarterly self-published journal commenting on design and pop culture, and launching 3ST.2, a new-media group. The bucolic setting can be misleading; Thirst is in motion, a blur to anyone who may be waving—or snarling—from the curb.

Rob Dewey is design director at the Minneapolis agency Hunt Adkins.

TURNING UP THE VOLUME

THE 1996 ANNUAL REPORT OF THE CHICAGO BOARD OF TRADE

07.12.96

CHICAGO BOARD OF TRADE ANNUAL REPORT_1997; 1999 (INSET)

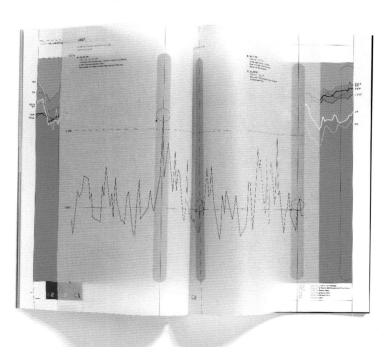

FT COLUMN: HISTORY; INDECISIONS; BUSINESS_1998; RIGHT COLUMN: PORTRAIT; CRISIS, DATA_1999

BACK THEN IT LOOKED LIKE THE KINGS WHO DESIGNED THE WHEEL WOULD ULTIMATELY BE FUELED BY GREED...

234
RV
LQV
WV

ILLUSTRATION FOR WIRED "FUTURE" ISSUE WITH CONCEPT SKETCH_1995

THE
DIVINE
dot.comEDY

A (Sad, But) True Story

Preſented in the Form of a Play in Two Parts

Part the Firſt:
"I Excel"

DRAMATIS PERSONÆ

ROB, *a writer and (confi)Dante*   BILL, *a president*

RICK, *a designer*   DAVE, *a vice president of marketing*

PATRIC, *a young designer*   BERT, *the chief executive officer*

THE CHORUS   THE GHOST OF TOM WATSON JR.

The Thirst office, a two-story house in the posh Chicago suburb of Barrington,

is represented onstage by a single young tree containing a bird's nest.

The tree reflects changes in season.

Rob's writer's studio is represented by a bust of the Roman poet Virgil.

All remaining settings except for the airplane – offices and the hotel – are represented by various clocks.

Otherwise, the stage is bare of decorative objects.

Time: The Recent Past

ACT ONE: SCENE I – IT BEGINS

The scene opens with Rick, seated at his computer in the Thirst office, composing an e-mail to Bill and his colleague Dave. Bill is the young, Ivy League–educated president of one of the world's largest web development roll-ups, iXL. Dave is the West Coast marketing genius credited with creating the infomercial and assigned to the road show preceding the company's initial public offering.

The story is true (at least this side of it).

RICK [*reading aloud as he types*]: To . . . Bill. Dave. Tab.

Cee cee . . . Rob. Tab.

Subject . . . *opportunity*, open brackets, *lost*, close brackets. Tab. Tab.

Let me take this missive to thank you for affording both myself and the entire Thirst community the opportunity to have been in your service. Return.

Yesterday was a very sad moment here when we opened an e-mail file from Frank Ford displaying the iXL signature direction to date. It seems unfortunate that you would mistake the act of change for change itself. Return.

I flashed back to the unifying words delivered by you, Bill, at the dinner table on the eve of the marketing summit. It was there you asked all of your guests for a *positioning* direction. Return.

The original iXL logo.

Two days later, you, Rob, and I had a most invigorating session in your office reviewing our recommendations related to the positioning of iXL. The essence of our noticing process identified the *real* positioning opportunity for a big web development consultancy like yours to actually be *smart*. *Big* equal sign *smart* is the unoccupied space ripe for someone like iXL to fill and retain over the long term. Return.

Gaining access to this space, however, requires an uncompromised visionary position. The world we practice in is already savvy enough to detect and dismiss the imitators at the front gate. Return.

On a personal level, I experienced a career high during that session with you. Your ThinkPad had just displayed our Java applet sketch of the new iXL dynamic identity idea. You turned back to me like a kid in a candy store and said, all caps, *that's fuckin' cool*. That moment will never be forgotten. In many ways that moment validates my belief, twenty-one professional years strong, that there are indeed people out there in decision-making positions who really *do see* the new, the next, and the now. Return.

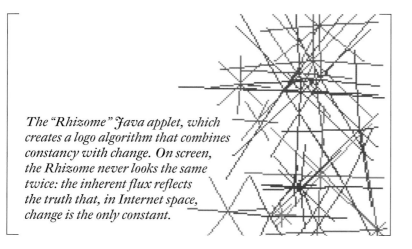

The "Rhizome" Java applet, which creates a logo algorithm that combines constancy with change. On screen, the Rhizome never looks the same twice: the inherent flux reflects the truth that, in Internet space, change is the only constant.

There was, and is, no doubt that the company you and Dave define is a company well poised to lead the industry and the communications renaissance. It is also clear that the two of you see that great design is great business. Open brackets.

It was the late Tom Watson Jr. who coined the phrase "good design is good business." [*Enter Ghost of Tom Watson Jr. in ethereal makeup, dressed like the visionary IBM CEO circa 1970. The Ghost stands behind Rick's chair in silence. Periodically, the Ghost pats Rick on the back.*] Close brackets. Return.

The Rhizome hand-rendered by an iXL employee.

At the top, the unspoken code among corporate leaders is the practiced understanding of this truth. Great design is great business. It truly has proven itself to be the secret sauce! Return.

To accent this position, let me point to a recent *Forbes* study that identified a handful of corporations leading the category of social responsibility. All of these model corporations have an intrinsic comprehension and display of this truth. Their top-down, total awareness of this truth is at the core of their real universal attraction, transcending the commercial boundaries of time and language.

Interestingly, Herman Miller. Open brackets, rated #1, close brackets. Coke. Open brackets, rated #2, close brackets. And DuPont. Open brackets, rated #3, close brackets. Are also extremely successful in attracting Wall Street. Return.

I will not go on rubbing salt in your wounds. Again, Thirst was proud of this opportunity and the new thinking it encouraged. Positioning iXL well into the future as the undisputed, most visionary, most passionate, unique provider of communications solutions, however, required more than just the recipe card. It required a belief in the universal truth at the most senior level! Return. [*Pauses to think.*]

Having not had an opportunity to go face to face with the chairman remains *my* personal regret. I would have had no lack of words or poise announcing to the emperor that he stands naked in front of a jury of his peers, silly-looking, vulnerable, and without a clue at the entrance to Augusta. Return.

Again, good luck. I am certain our paths will cross again as we share the future's space. Return.

Rick Valicenti. Send.

[*Rick triumphantly presses the enter key, launching the e-mail. He then leans back in his chair, hands behind his head. Lights fade.*]

@~

ACT ONE: SCENE II – SECRET REBELS IN THE CORPORATE BOSOM

On stage stands Rob. A single dim spotlight on him gradually flares up to a blinding white beam.

ROB: They're out there. That's what drives you nuts. They really are out there. The cool people who [*momentarily forming finger quotation marks*] "get" design . . . and some of them are even in the big companies. They're in the offices and cubicles with the cool posters . . . protected from blah-ness by a force field of cool imagery . . . they have the breathtaking screen savers . . . the interesting books stored on the standard-issue company bookshelves.

[*Rob pauses to light a cigarette with a wooden match, which he deliberately removes from a box. After he lights the cigarette, he lets the match burn down.*] These are the secret rebels. They nurture their design teams.

They console themselves with cool music. [*Blows out match.*]

They learned about Thirst at school . . . or at design conferences . . . or on awards lists or coffee-table anthologies. [*Longer pause.*]

Sometimes they pick up the phone.

@~

ACT ONE: SCENE III – WHY DO WE DO IT? PART I

Enter Chorus, consisting of a thirty-something woman, an adolescent boy, and an adolescent girl. On the boy's hand is a baseball glove. The girl wears a tiara. The woman, fully dressed save for a blouse (she wears a bra), holds the children's hands. The Chorus circumambulates the stage casually, as if visiting a museum or zoo.

ROB [*in a slightly raised voice*]: After so many disappointments, so many cool designs turned bland by client fear, why do we do it? I joke with Rick about it. Are we so needy – do we have such low self-esteem – that we seek out abusive relationships?

CHORUS: Why?

ROB: So many reasons . . . mutually contradictory . . . that don't add up.

CHORUS: Why?

ROB: In part because of the siren song of history. Leafing through that Paul Rand book will put that weird fire of ambition in your guts . . . make you drop your guard . . . make it seem worth the risk.

CHORUS: Why?

ROB: In part . . . because I am still a sucker for the attention of the big shot . . . just like a ninth grader in the pit orchestra talking to the female lead of the high school musical . . . [*scowls slightly*] even though she's only flirting with me to piss off her boyfriend. So having a *high official* from a *name company* come a-courtin' still makes my heart race, despite myself.

CHORUS: Why?